Making Ev

With the Teachings of Rebbe Nachman of Breslov

May You Have a Day

Chaya Rivka Zwolinski

Table of Contents

This book is dedicated to Gavriel and Chana Sneider.
May this book be a merit for them as they continue
spreading the teachings of Rebbeinu Nachman ben
Faiga. May they be blessed with a long life filled with
joy, closeness to Hashem and the Tzaddik Emes.

"Rejoice, Zevulun, in your departure, and
Yissaschar, in your tents." (Devarim 33:18)

To "Izzy",

May we always find joy in our partnership and our work.
May our joy and hard work, with Hashem's
help, lead to great things.

With much gratitude,
"Zevy"

With tremendous gratitude to Chaya Rivka Zwolinski

The Franks Family

Dedicated in memory of my father,
Daniel ben Yosef Goldberg
And in honor of my mother, Ettel bas
Zalman (Ethel) Goldberg

From their loving daughter,
Shulamit Michal (Susan) Strassburger

For our dear friends, Chana and Gavriel Sneider,
May you be blessed with always-
increasing *emunah* and *bitachon*,

Rachelle and Larry Ellis

With gratitude to Hashem, may this be a merit
for our family members who came before and will
come after (please G-d). Also dedicated to Chaya
Rivka Zwolinski (until 120 in good health) and BRI,
who share the profound teachings of our Torah and
its spiritual masters. Thank you for strengthening
our bond with Hashem and each other.

❤❤ Janice and Shira Chana Bienstock

Breslov Woman and the author dedicate this book:

L'iluy Nishmat Cheena Rochel bas Chaim Menachem

In Honor of Gavriel and Chana Sneider,
May they be blessed with success, joy, and Tsfat

In Honor of the Huggins Family

In Honor of Richard and Bea Greenberg

In Honor of Miriam Marika Frohlinger,
May she go from strength to strength

In loving memory and gratitude to my beloved
paternal grandparents, Bessie and Charles Kazansky,
OBM, whose beautifully simple observance of
Judaism set my heart aflame with intense yearning
and love for Hashem and all His ways.

May this dedication be an Aliyah for their neshamos.

Hinda Kazansky

Dedicated with appreciation to Chaya
Rivka bas Yocheved Kayla
for helping me through difficult times.

Bina bat Farahnaz

Introduction

The world has changed dramatically. Now more than ever there is a sense of urgency in the search for the deeper meaning of life. More people than ever before are reflecting on the purpose of life and are looking for the missing pieces. More people than ever want to "get it right."

Do you yearn to uncover the deeper meaning behind the mundane? Do you feel that something is missing for you? Are you waiting for things to happen which you believe will bring positive change and happiness to your life? Are you unsure what a sense of completeness and joy really feels like?

Sometimes, personal growth seems forced on us from the outside. We all face so many challenging life circumstances. A crisis pulls us in two directions and we choose what we hope is the right choice. Maybe we follow old patterns. Maybe we are shown a new way and we have the once-in-a-lifetime chance to choose a fresh start over stasis. But how do we really know what the right life choices are? And how do we develop an authentic self that is capable of making these choices?

And what do we do during the times where our days are so ordinary (and comfortable), that if we want to grow, we have to push ourselves to feel motivated?

Like you, I wanted a happier life. I sometimes felt stuck in the quicksand of my emotions. I looked around and found fault with the world, yet I knew in my heart that any change in my life would have to begin with me. Yet how could I evaluate myself and make necessary changes while staying true to me?

Through a series of incredible events, I came to find the life-changing wisdom of Rebbe Nachman of Breslov.

The 18th century Hasidic master, Rebbe Nachman, teaches: Don't get too attached to the image of yourself that you have today, because the essence of being alive is constant growth. You not only can grow – you must grow! Look at your soul in the mirror and work to refine your being. You not only can change – you must change! Like a fish which has to keep moving to stay alive, you too have to live a life in constant spiritual motion, swimming through life's challenges, sometimes going with the current, and sometimes pushing upstream.

The teachings of Rebbe Nachman show me, as they've shown thousands of other people, how to be more resilient. They've shown me how to strengthen my faith and trust in God, but also how to believe in myself. They also show me how to cope with my imperfections and falls, without beating myself to smithereens. And they can show you, too.

For over a decade I've been teaching what I learned and am still learning. Through my work with the Breslov Research Institute, I began taking groups of women to visit the sites of Rebbe Nachman and the early Chassidim in Ukraine. In 2018 I began a WhatsApp daily mini-podcast about Rebbe Nachman's teachings. Those lessons became the foundation for this book and the continuing series,

May You Have a Day, IyH. In it, I take the complex topics that have changed my life, and make them accessible.

My suggestion is that you choose a particular short lesson in this book and think about it for a day or two, or even longer. Rebbe Nachman told us to "go with his lessons" for a few months. Often these lessons offer many different ideas as gateways into a unifying concept. The mini-lessons in *May You Have a Day* are based on Rebbe Nachman's lessons, distilled to offer one or two simple ideas that you can easily apply to your life. A small change is all it takes! As Rebbe Nachman says: A little bit is also good. My hope is that you find the short lessons in this book meaningful, practical and ready to be part of your real life.

May this journey lead you to many joyful days, days filled with faith, hope and inspiration. May it lead to positive change. May you have a day filled with light and blessing.

Chaya Rivka Zwolinski
Nissan 5780
April 2020

Starting Over

R ebbe Nachman teaches that we should pay no attention to our own conception of ourselves, especially if that conception is negative. If you find that you are limited by your idea of who you are, throw that idea out the window!

Understand: *Every day you are an entirely new creation.*

A person is created anew each and every day. Believe you can start over. Know you can start over. You can start over next week or tomorrow, and you can even start over again today. Start over as many times as you want or need. Why not start over now, this moment in time? Take a deep breath and start over.

If you're feeling down and your thoughts are in a negative spiral, start over.

If you tried to control your temper and failed, start over.

If you meant to be kinder and forgot, start over.

Rebbe Nachman tells us that no good thought is ever lost. Thoughts have their own lives and your good thoughts still exist in the spiritual realm where thoughts live. No thought ever needs to go to waste.

Find a good thought. Think back to the time when you had a good thought about your life, about God, about yourself. Remember that good thought. Go back in your mind. Retrieve that positive thought about yourself and refresh yourself with the positive concept you had of yourself in the past. Really, think this thought right now. With this thought in your mind, you can start anew.

May you have a day of fresh, new beginnings.

Confab with The Creator (Being Real)

Rebbe Nachman teaches us to talk to God every day, in our own words, just as we'd talk to our very best friend. If this is possible, when we speak to the Creator, are there rules? What are you allowed to talk about? Is any topic off the table? Are you allowed to express grief, loss, anger, and other unpleasant feelings? Is it okay to express what's on your mind and in your heart?

Or is it best to fake it and say, no matter how you really feel: "God, I know whatever I am going through is coming from you. I know if it's from you that it must be good. I should accept it and be grateful for it."

The truth is that not everyone can do this. In fact, most people can't do this, at least not all the time. It's hard to pretend to be happy when you aren't. So, what do you do? *The answer lies in remembering why we talk to God in the first place.*

Talking to God is so precious and valuable because He knows you better than anyone else. He is always with you. Whatever you are going through, whatever struggles, pain, heartache, fear, whatever your situation is, He already understands what you are feeling.

Now He wants *you* to understand what you are feeling, so you can work through it.

He wants you to know that He is there for you. He wants you to be able to understand that He is your best friend who knows and loves you (no matter what.)

This is what Rebbe Nachman says: *Talk to God as you would talk to your absolute best friend.*

Your best friend is always there for you when you need to vent, complain, and figure out uncomfortable feelings. It's okay to be honest and to be real with your emotions. It is also good to express gratitude and appreciation and thank God even for the hard things in life.

Think about this – it's a *mitzvah* to listen to someone else share her troubles. You're there for your friends and family, right? You know that when a person shares her troubles, her burden becomes lighter. So why can't God do this *mitzvah* for *you*? Will He listen to you while you share your troubles? The tzaddikim tell us He will.

If you're going through a hard time, don't beat yourself up just because you feel an urge to express your discomfort or pain. You've got enough on your plate. It's okay. Be real. Tell God exactly how you are feeling. You're allowed. It doesn't mean you are going to permanently wallow in that state. It does mean that you're honest and you're real and you're human.

May you have a day where you can open up your heart to God.

The Top Prize

How do we know what's truly a meaningful accomplishment? Developing and using our gifts and talents is certainly commendable. But in the following story, Rebbe Nachman shows that our choices, especially the difficult ones including those about our commitments, may be even more valuable than coming out on top.

Once upon a time there was a king who used to send secret messages to his ally, another king in a nearby country, by way of special messengers. The messengers would memorize the king's messages, travel to the other king, and then relay the message once they were secluded with him.

In order to get to the other king, the messengers had to pass through a hostile kingdom. The hostile king was the sworn enemy of the two friendly kings, and he was always suspicious of them and on the lookout for any whiff of conspiracy.

One day the first king sent out his most elite, intelligent messenger. This messenger wore a brilliant disguise and blended in with the populace. He got through the hostile kingdom and was able to deliver his message to the friendly king.

Soon the king needed to send another message. He chose another elite messenger, one who was extremely strong. He also passed through the neighboring kingdom. However, just as he was about to get through, the enemy king's soldiers caught him. They put him in solitary confinement, planning to return later to torture him. Before they returned, this messenger was able to bend the bars of his jail cell and escape. He scaled the wall and jumped, ran swiftly through the enemy territory, and successfully delivered the message to the king.

The king needed to send a third message but his top messengers were resting after their successful forays. He chose another messenger. He wasn't as intelligent as the first messenger nor as strong as the second. As he entered the enemy kingdom he was caught right away. This time the enemy king's soldiers didn't risk an escape—they began torturing him immediately. But this messenger didn't give in. Then they offered him a lot of money and a position in the hostile king's court if he would reveal the secret message, but he didn't give in no matter how much wealth and honor they promised him. He just said over and over again: "I don't know anything". Finally, the soldiers decided he really didn't know anything and let him go. Eventually he was able to deliver his message and return home.

The king decided to reward his messengers for their hard work. He called all his ministers together to discuss which of these three messengers should get the highest reward. Some argued that the first messenger was so smart he hadn't even been caught, so he deserved the top prize. Others argued that the second messenger certainly deserved the top prize since even though he was captured, he used all his strength to make a brilliant escape. But the king decided to give the top prize to the third messenger. True, he got caught. True, he was tortured. But he was most deserving, decided the king, because he held out under torture and refused all offers of wealth and honor in his loyalty to the king.

Rebbe Nachman teaches that intelligence and strength are gifts. Were you born smart or at least had the gift of intellectual potential? Were you born physically strong or given the capacity to have a strong body? Far better to be steadfast and to hang on to the truth, than to have brilliance or strength. Hanging on to your commitment to the king, now this is your choice. This is a genuine achievement. This deserves the greatest reward, the top prize.

May you have a day in which you strengthen your commitment to spiritual growth.

Beginning with Prayer

Rebbe Nachman said that people will wait until they are at the end of their ropes before they pray. They will change their diets. They will go to doctors. They will fill in dozens of job applications. They'll go for a jog or to the gym. They'll rack their brains, have long complicated arguments, and even temper tantrums. People will do anything and everything to solve their predicament – except pray. Only when they can't take it anymore, then they will pray. Then they'll talk to God and ask for His Help.

Rebbe Nachman told us to do the opposite. He says: *Begin with prayer.* When you begin with prayer you are showing that you believe that God is the source of everything. You are demonstrating that He is the only address where you can find salvation.

We think of habits as negative things. But some habits are good. You can get into the habit of turning to God first, before you take action. If you do, you may end up standing taller, feeling stronger, and seeing solutions sooner.

May you have a day in which you turn to God first.

Leaving the Exile of Depression

R eb Noson explains that exile and depression are related to each other. When a person is going through a hard time (a physical illness, financial worry, or any other suffering), it's easy to fall into depression. Depression is synonymous with exile. When we're depressed, we're in exile.

The *Kabbalah* teaches that the *Shechinah*, the feminine, hidden aspect of the Holy One, is also in exile. Both the *Shechinah's* exile and our own, mirror each other. But there is only one way we can depart exile – and that's with joy. When we choose to live life with more joy, we begin to take ourselves out of exile. When we choose to connect to *Hashem* with joy, we not only lift ourselves out of our own depression-exile, but we lift out the *Shechinah* from her exile, too. The more joyful we are, the more we help to release and reveal the *Shechinah*. When She is fully revealed, the redemption has come. Then, everyone will know Hashem and the earth will be filled with light and love.

May you have a day in which you heal your depression with joy.

Correcting Others

Some people want to fix other people and correct them. It's part of their nature. Sometimes, this is genuinely well-meaning. After all, we're taught that giving *tochacha*, moral correction, is a great *mitzvah* and technically an obligation for each of us. But in actuality, says Rebbe Nachman, this is something we should avoid.

He explains that most of us don't have the necessary insight into how to correct someone effectively. When we do attempt *tochacha*, we tend to focus on the wrong aspects of correction. Instead of focusing on the person's strengths, we focus on the flaws, the consequence of which is that we weaken the soul of the person we are trying to correct. We forget that the idea is to build people up, not shame or humiliate them.

Chassidism is all about lifting people up. At the time the Baal Shem Tov founded the Chassidic movement in the early 1700s, itinerant preachers would travel from town to town giving sermons. They were hired by local congregations. In each town they would dramatically rebuke the congregants from the pulpit. They would shame them and make them feel so down about their transgressions that the people would cry and tremble in fear. When they were totally beaten down and hopeless, the preacher's job was done, and he moved on to the next town.

The Baal Shem Tov saw that this was not helping people. To put down people who were already struggling, who were trying to scrape by in a very hostile environment, was a grave injustice in the Baal Shem Tov's eyes. He had a great love for the Jewish people and this situation caused him a lot of heartache. It also was one of the things that inspired him to give life to the *Chassidic* movement, which offered a way to lift people up and bring them closer to God – with sweetness and joy.

The great-grandson of the Baal Shem Tov, Rebbe Nachman of Breslov, teaches that only a *tzaddik* knows how to give moral rebuke. The *tochacha* from a *tzaddik* nourishes the soul and doesn't weaken it. Why? Because a *tzaddik* lovingly lasers in on the person's good points.

In many of his lessons, Rebbe Nachman of Breslov teaches us how to motivate and inspire others. But first he teaches us how to motivate, inspire and believe in ourselves. The best way to begin is by recognizing our own good points, clearing our own path so we can build a joyful connection to God.

May you have a day in which you are able to see
the good points in yourself and others.

7

Talk Your Way to Greatness

Rebbe Nachman's most famous piece of advice is concerning private secluded prayer. This is a talking meditation-prayer in which we speak to the Creator in our own words about whatever is on our mind and in our heart. This private conversation is called *hitbodedut*. *Hitbodedut* doesn't have to be overly complicated. It is a matter of setting aside a certain amount of time daily to be alone with God.

If you are new to *hitbodedut* and are only able to set aside a few minutes at first, that is fine. Just do it. Set aside a few minutes a day to speak to *Hashem* honestly about your troubles and worries. Tell Him what you are grateful for as well as the things you need more of in your life. Tell Him about your regrets and sorrows. Ask Him to help you come closer to Him. Whatever is on your mind, just start talking to *Hashem*.

Rebbe Nachman says *hitbodedut* is how the great *tzaddikim* became great *tzaddikim*. It will help you become great, too. Remember that each day is a new beginning. You can always start over. In *hitbodedut* you can say, "*Hashem*, today I am starting to attach myself to you. Today I am renewing my relationship with you. Please help me. Help me speak to you honestly. Help me come close to you. Opening your heart to *Hashem* will bring you solace, relief, and joy. It will help you find your personal best.

May you have a day in which you see the
blessings talking to God can bring.

Alive Today

Rebbe Nachman tells us that all you have is today. Yesterday can drag you down. You can get caught up in memories that may confuse, confound and depress you. Then, you'll be filled with regret. Or you might dream about tomorrow. Then you'll get caught up in fantasies that may or may not come to pass. You'll be living in a make-believe world.

Focus on the present. Stay in the moment. Say: I am going to accomplish *now*. I am going to accomplish *today*. Then you'll achieve. Although this holds true in all life's areas, it holds especially true for spiritual matters. Focus on the present and you'll find it easier to come closer to God and connect to Him.

Tomorrow, says Rebbe Nachman, is an entirely new world. It's an entirely new creation. Today is the moment you have in which to fully live.

May you have a day in which you are aware of each moment.

Where Can I Find the Solutions to My Problems?

n *Likutey Moharan* 195, Rebbe Nachman discusses the troubles and problems people face. He discusses how you can step outside of your instinctive reactions and reframe your experiences. When you do, you will come to understand your problems quite differently.

In Psalms 4:2, King David says: "In the midst of my troubles You relieved me." Rebbe Nachman explains that when trouble strikes, God relieves us. Even by means of the trouble itself, God relieves us. Even when we're totally bogged down with suffering, we can find a key to unlock a solution. The problem itself contains the salvation. Sometimes we can even come to see the terrible thing we're dealing with as a salvation itself.

Ask yourself:

Is my problem bringing me closer to God?

Is my problem forcing me to learn about myself?

Is my problem challenging me and helping me grow?

Of course, when people suffer, you naturally yearn to comfort them. God also yearns to comfort you. He is always there to comfort you, even though this might be hard to feel at first. At the same time, when you are going through hard times, if you go deeper, look within, and look for God inside the troubles themselves – with faith and persistence, you will find His light, love and comfort.

May you have a day where you are aware that
the Holy One yearns to comfort you.

Secret to Long Life

Rebbe Nachman tells us the secret to long life: *In order to ensure that we have "a long life", we need to become aware of each day, each hour, and even each moment.* When we're aware of the amount of time we've been given, we can grab that portion of time and pack it full of holiness.

For example, let's say you're awake for eighteen hours a day. During every single one of those hours you can take thirty seconds, sixty seconds (or more) and make a conscious choice to do a *mitzvah* or good deed. It takes just part of a minute. Give *tzedakah*. Pray. Help someone out. Learn a little lesson from the *tzaddikim*. Say a blessing over what you are eating. Little by little, you'll find you're making more and more choices like these. You'll get in the habit. You'll pack your moments with spiritually uplifting thoughts and positive actions.

If you are determined enough, and you stick with this for a while, you'll see this becomes much easier. Eventually, you'll find that your days feel longer, richer and fuller. *This is the secret to having a long life.* When every day is filled with more holiness than the day before, you will be blessed with length of days. Long days are long life.

May you have a day packed with holiness.

Make A Vessel for Blessing

Rebbe Nachman explains in *Likutey Moharan* 76 that when you trust in God utterly and look only to Him for all your needs, a vessel is formed with which you can receive His blessings. What you need will be sent to you. This is a very high level of *bitachon*, trust.

What is trust, really? Trust is applied *emunah*. We have faith in our hearts and minds but we show that we really do trust by our actions. Often, the more we trust in God the less we feel we have to take action. We have faith in God and trust that he will provide us with our paycheck, our food, our shelter. But the way of the world is that we must take some action. We don't sleep until noon and wait for our car payments to fall from the sky. We go to work. Action and *emunah* and *bitachon* build our blessings-vessel.

Our faith and trust help us be at peace when someone else gets the promotion we wanted, because we trust that the Holy One decided this wasn't the best thing for us right now. We don't work too much overtime because we know that we need time for family, prayer, learning and joy. In ordinary times we don't take extraordinary measures to "make a living." We know that God wants us to work a reasonable amount and have time for other important things.

In general, the higher a person's level of *emunah* and *bitachon*, the less action he needs to take in order to receive God's bounty. How do we make this internal shift? Begin by focusing your thoughts on making the shift and then talking to the Creator about it. Ask for His help: "God, how do I learn to trust you to send me everything I need? Help me Hashem, I want to trust in you!"

You can encourage friends and family to learn *emunah* and *bitachon* right along with you. When others in your life feel the way you do, it will reinforce what you're learning.

You can also develop faith and trust by looking at what you already have in your life. Look at how God has sustained you until this point. When you're going through a tough time, you might easily forget that many of your needs (if not most), have been fulfilled in the past and are being fulfilled in the present. You probably have shelter and food and clothing. You have family and friends, or at least one good friend. All or most of your body parts do their jobs. Your brain is able to think and reflect. When you consider what God has sent you over the course of your life, this increases your ability to live with trust.

*May you be blessed with a day where you
trust, believe, and hope in God.*

What the Tzaddikim Teach Us

Reb Noson, Rebbe Nachman's leading follower and scribe, teaches us something about the great *tzaddikim*. When we think of our righteous sages and teachers, we think of their holiness and their spiritual devotions. Reb Noson says they have another quality that is also valuable. This is their lifetime experience of spiritual ascents and descents.

Because they have been successful and they have come out on top spiritually, they are experts at knowing how to navigate life's ups and downs. The *tzaddikim* give us advice about dealing with life's roller coaster; what to do and when to do it. They show us how to rise up if we are down, and how to temper the complacency that often comes when we reach the top.

The true *tzaddikim* transmit to us instructions on how to strengthen ourselves in all situations. They help us develop personalized healthy thought patterns and behaviors that become life-long skills. If we pay attention to the teachings of the true *tzaddikim* and especially the *tzaddik*, Rebbe Nachman, if we learn these teachings and make them our own, we'll find they literally pick us up from the darkest spiritual nights and bring us to a higher place than we could ever have imagined.

May you have a day in which you navigate life's ups and downs with your personal psychospiritual strength.

Walking

Rebbe Nachman teaches that everyone must try to develop proficiency in *halacha*, the Jewish codes of law. These are the codes which show us how to connect to God. The word *halacha* is related to *halicha*, which means "to walk."

Similarly, in *Likutey Moharan* 6, Rebbe Nachman explains that a person must try to develop proficiency in knowing when to walk forward in life and when it's better to just sit and wait. When you are trying to come closer to God, to connect to Him and grow spiritually, you must try and understand some things about the path you're on.

One day, sometime after you begin your journey, you will find obstacles spring up. The obstacles may be frustrating, embarrassing, and sometimes even painful. Questions will arise: "Are the obstacles a sign that I'm on the wrong path? Are these obstacles insurmountable? Should I just give up on coming closer to God?" The questions might build and without thoughtful understanding, you could fall into an existential crisis and feel deeply discouraged. If this happens, you might even stop trying. You might give up.

Rebbe Nachman says: *Don't give up!* He encourages us to learn what to do so that we are strengthened and not diminished. He also shows us how to encourage ourselves. When we follow his advice, we gain insight and learn when to walk forward and when it's okay to just sit a bit and hold our place. Sometimes we have to sit still, spirituality speaking. Sometimes we have to forge ahead. In this way we live our lives in balance. When we know when and how to walk, we are then truly able to enter into a life of holiness.

May you have a day in which you know when it's
time to go forward and when it's time to sit.

One True Word, One True Heart

R eb Noson explains that there are times when a person can say the entire daily prayer service but he can't salvage even one word. Every word is a dry, empty, lifeless husk. This can go on for an entire day. Sometimes it can go on for weeks or months. Then suddenly, one time, his heart is moved. He cries out one word from the very depth of his soul. This one, true word is so powerful it literally saves all the rest of his prayers, those that were dead until that point. It brings them to life, like a defibrillator.

Sometimes your prayers might feel like a mere husk, filled with a lot of hot air and little else. You may not be able to concentrate or if you do, you're not so interested in what you're saying. You can barely get through them. You force yourself, but nothing is clicking. You might feel you are the only person in the world with this problem, you might feel like everyone else is more sincere or holier than you, but that's just not true. Everyone goes through this sometimes.

Rebbe Nachman says no matter what, we still should say our daily written prayers. We should also make an effort to speak to God in *hitbodedut*, too. Even if it feels like nothing is happening, the mere fact that you are moving your lips is still valuable. Your commitment to making time to pray still counts.

Don't worry – if you can't muster up feelings of inspiration, just know that if you keep trying, eventually you will be able to cry out in truth. It might not happen when you think you are on a high spiritual level. It might happen that one day you slip, you fall and stumble in spiritual matters. You feel you sunk to a low level and feel ashamed. This shame can activate your heart! Your heart of stone cracks and you find you are able to pray so authentically, so wholeheartedly, you never want to stop talking to God.

May you have a day where you pray with hope and truth.

How to Avoid
Anger & Conflict

I n *Likutey Moharan* 56, Rebbe Nachman teaches that *Shalom*, complete peace, depends on *da'at*, authentic knowledge and the holy awareness that the Creator is in charge. When we don't have *da'at*, we don't have *Shalom*.

Without *da'at* we become mired down in battles. Conflict and controversy plague us. We pick fights. We respond to the slightest of slights that people may casually toss our way. We become confused about what we are doing with our lives. We think we need to be activists. We think we need to fight every battle that comes our way. But in truth, we don't. We need to focus on building ourselves and building up the positive relationships in our lives.

Rebbe Nachman says that when a person doesn't have the holy awareness that everything comes from the Creator, she is going to be involved in fights. When a person understands the limitations of human intellect, she makes a space for *da'at* to begin to blossom. When she realizes that human understanding of justice is limited, she suddenly will realize that anger is a disgrace. Arguments are a disgrace. Why be angry if we're not in charge?

The Rebbe teaches that in general, it's better to let things go, even when you're right, than to engage in conflict. It's true that as people age, they tend to want to get involved in fewer and fewer arguments. More young people are hot-headed activists. Still, even if you're young, think about the big picture. The Rebbe tells us it is better to start working on our psychospiritual growth when we're young. He says it's good to remember what you're really supposed to be doing here in this lifetime. Then anger and conflict will pass you by.

May you have a day of holy awareness and peaceful relationships.

True Prayer Always Helps

Rebbe Nachman teaches that prayer helps with *everything*. It helps bring us closer to God. It helps us feel more positive about our lives. It helps with important life-quality issues including health, monetary success, and relief from fear and worry. It gives us the strength to solve the problems we encounter in life. It helps solves problems with relationships, marriage and children. Whatever it is that's bothering you, prayer helps.

It's best if the prayer is genuine, the kind of prayer that comes from the heart with a lot of faith and belief. Perhaps you may think you uttered heartfelt prayers in the past and saw that your prayers weren't answered. While it's true that sometimes you might pray from the heart and don't see exactly what you are praying for, if you look closely, you will see that there was at least some relief in your situation. Think back to a time in your life when you prayed and you saw an answer or a solution, or even a little bit of relief materialized. Tap into that power of the way you prayed back then and reinvigorate your prayers today.

May you have a day of fresh prayer.

17

Think About Joy

Rebbe Nachman says: *Know yourself! Know what makes you tick!* Sit down for five minutes a day (or two minutes a day) and think about where you are headed and what you want out of life. Make the head space and the heart space to think about taking a break from the oppressive, mundane worries you have.

Rebbe Nachman says: *Make yourself joyful!*

We all know what gives us pleasure and momentary happiness. But do you know yourself well enough to know what gives you lasting joy? This requires serious thought. Meditation (focused thought), is essential if you want to fulfill your life mission and joy is an integral part of how you fulfill it. Take the time to think about what makes you truly joyful. It may be your children or grandchildren. It may be going for a walk in a beautiful natural setting and talking to God. It may be singing songs on Shabbat or listening to music, or dancing. It may be having a heartfelt conversation or learning a little Breslov with your spouse. It may be going for a run! It may be something lofty or complex or much simpler.

Whatever it is, make your joy your own. Make it a priority that you find moments of joy in every day. With joy you can come closer to true self-actualization. With joy you can activate your soul and come closer to God.

May you have a day where you tap into your power of personal joy.

18

See the Good in Others

Rebbe Nachman says that we should turn our eyes away from seeing what's wrong with everyone else. We shouldn't look at their misbehavior, their errors and their flaws. We should instead focus on what is good about others. And, just to make this more difficult, there's a requirement—we must make no exception for people with whom we have arguments. We must look for the good even in them. Especially in them! It's not just a Breslov way – *this is the Jewish way*. We are supposed to love each other.

There's a shortcut to achieving this. Simply identify and focus only on what is lovable in the other person. When you ignore someone's shortcomings and laser in on what's good about him or her, you end up having a better relationship. Even if you're in conflict with that person, or having an argument, even if all you can do is just walk away from the argument with one positive thought in your mind, you're better off. The obvious reason why it's important to focus on the good in others is so that you avoid hatred, strife and conflict.

Feeling negatively about other people is draining. It distracts you from doing what you should be doing, which is building up other people, building up your closeness to God, and building up yourself.

May you have a day where seeing the good in others comes easily.

19

Compromise

Rebbe Nachman speaks about the value of compromise. He compares it to giving *tzedakah*, charity. *Tzedakah* is related to *tzedek* which means righteousness. *Tzedek* also means doing the right thing. When we give charity, God gives us the money that indeed belongs to us. Yet, it's up to us to spend it appropriately. It's up to us to distribute it to others who are materially or spiritually needy.

Compromise is similar. At times, we have a disagreement with someone or we want to do something and someone else doesn't want to go along with us. When we yield for the sake of peace it's like giving a part of ourselves, something that belongs to us, for the sake of peace. Compromise doesn't mean that we compromise our deep-seated Jewish values or morals. But conflict over these authentic Jewish values is not as common as you might think. In the vast majority of disagreements, it's not a question of upholding the Torah. In the long run, the argument really isn't that important. At these times, aim for peace.

It's true there are times when we may need to be unyielding. But remember: Rebbe Nachman himself never pushed. He never forced an issue. He allowed people to be who they needed to be and to do what they needed to do. He himself was known for avoiding conflicts whenever possible. Compromising, making peace, this is a fundamental way of expressing *Ahavat Yisrael*, love of your brothers and sisters. It's a truly sweet way to give charity.

May you have a day of righteous compromise.

20

Is Fashion Spiritual?

I n *Megillat Esther*, the scroll we read during the holiday of Purim, it's written that Esther was forced to join the harem of the evil king Ahasuerus. Mordechai, her Uncle, was worried about her, so he would walk every day in front of the courtyard of the harem in order to find out how she was doing. He would eavesdrop on the women's conversations and learn how his niece fared.

The Holy *Zohar* teaches that Esther personifies the *Shechinah*, the hidden, feminine aspect of God, also known as the Divine Presence. Mordechai was learning how the *Shechinah* was faring. In *Likutey Moharan* 203, Rebbe Nachman teaches that from women's conversations it's possible to learn the state of the *Shechinah*.

The *Zohar* teaches that the *Shechinah* constantly changes her garments. What she wears in the morning she doesn't wear in the evening. This changing of the *Shechinah's* garments reflects the changing status of what us human beings are up to, whether we are doing a lot of *mitzvot* and good deeds, or the opposite. Incredibly, the things we do affect and are reflected by the *Shechinah*! When we move in a positive direction, the *Shechinah* is positively affected. Of course, the opposite is true.

From this we understand the deeper meaning of women's conversations. There is no shame that for women, fashion is often a topic – what's in style, what's on sale, what we like and don't like, and so on. These seemingly mundane discussions, like the ones Mordechai listened to, have a deeper meaning. We may not be aware of the deeper meanings of our words, when we speak about clothing, careers, recipes, children, etc., but that doesn't mean that these conversations are without value.

Remember, we are usually not aware of the deeper meanings even when we're speaking about *Torah, Chassidut*, and other spiritual topics. No matter what you're doing, hidden mysteries abound. Even if you're not aware, you remain connected to God. Keep in mind: Your conversations about mundane things like clothing are a glimpse into the state of beloved Divine Presence! Remember this no matter what you talk about, and you'll instinctively raise the quality of your conversations. When you elevate your speech in even your everyday conversations, you reflect a more positive reality and bring this positivity to the *Shechinah*.

May you have a day in which all your
conversations are uplifting and kind.

21

Your New Self

ebbe Nachman tells us that our service of God, our mitzvot, and the good deeds we do, are like our children. Before a woman gives birth, she has to undergo contractions and birth pangs. She cries and she screams. Before we can truly connect to God, before we can rise to a new spiritual level, we have to undergo spiritual contractions and birth pangs. We cry and we scream.

It's so difficult to take ourselves to that next level. It's a kind of giving birth. And not only are we giving birth to a new version of ourselves, but we are also giving birth to positive new energies in this world. Don't be discouraged if things are difficult when you want to grow. Challenge yourself and believe you can do it. Don't let the difficulties discourage you – hang in there. Endure it. Take some deep breaths. Ignore the suffering and focus on the outcome. The outcome will be a new you and a better world.

May you have a day in which you believe in your innate ability to go higher no matter what you're facing.

More Than Angels

Rebbe Nachman tells us something amazing about people. He explains that the Holy One, has many kinds of *malachim*, angels. There are varieties of angels called *seraphim, chayot,* and *ophanim.* There are myriad angels. The entire purpose of these angelic Heavenly beings is to sing the Creator's praises in the upper worlds, and do His will. Yet, the thing that gives God the most pleasure and joy is when a simple person like you or me, yearns to connect with Him; when a person makes even a small effort to connect with Him.

You and I are just simple human beings. We're not angels. We're a mixed bag. There are some good points to us. There are some not good points to us. Yet when we reach deep inside ourselves, we can rise above our everyday lives. When we reach for Hashem, we bring the Creator of the Universe pleasure and joy. God gives us this power to bring Him joy – what an incredible power! This is evidence of His love for us.

May you have a day in which you give the Creator joy.

23

What We Want

I n *Likutey Moharan* 20, Rebbe Nachman tells us that whenever we pray, we shouldn't try to force things. We shouldn't insist that God does exactly what we want Him to do.

Rebbe Nachman tells us that we can request whatever we want. We can ask God to show us His love in a way we can understand. If God gives us what we request, that's great. If not, the Rebbe says we should accept this, too.

The Rebbe explains that God has many ways of helping us. God's Wisdom is not our wisdom. It's possible that true help isn't going to come the way we imagine it will come. Have you ever asked for something in your life and not received it? Later you find yourself reflecting back on that situation and realize, "Thank God that back then, I didn't get what I thought I needed! It would have been so terrible if it had come true."

Still, the only address to turn to when you do need something is the Holy One.

*May you have a day in which your prayers
are heard and answered.*

24

Learning Hope

I n *Likutey Moharan* 18 Rebbe Nachman explains that everything
in creation has a goal and a purpose. The ultimate goal of creation is the delight of *Olam HaBa,* the World to Come, and the
experience of being close to God. No one can really understand or
grasp this goal except the *tzaddikim.* This is why it's so important
that we have a connection to the *tzaddikim,* especially the *tzaddik
emes,* Rebbe Nachman. Through this connection, we begin to get
a glimmer of what this holy experience must be like.

When we become connected to the *tzaddik* we become more compassionate, too. The *tzaddik* teaches us compassion by demonstrating
his own compassion. We begin to view ourselves through the mirror
of the *tzaddik's* teachings, and gain compassion for ourselves (and
others.) Compassion leads to hope. To sense the sweetness of the
ultimate goal – this is what makes life a fulfilling delight.

May you have a day in which you build your
bond with the true tzaddikim.

25

Shattering Anger

n *Likutey Moharan* 18 Rebbe Nachman tells us that we must learn to break our anger with mercy. We should tap into the power of compassion and mercy in order to nullify our natural cruelty. That's not something we want to know about, this innate cruelty, but the truth is we might have a knee-jerk cruel response to certain situations.

Sometimes we get angry and it's obvious. We feel like screaming or yelling or making biting remarks to someone. We may try to restrain ourselves, and whether or not we attack or hold back, matters. Still, even the unexpressed feeling of anger or the wish to "get back" at someone is poison.

Anger is often one parasitic strangling vine in a jungle of feelings. It feeds off fear or jealousy. We think, "Hey, that person has something (status, love, knowledge, money) that I don't. If they have it, there won't be any left for me." This is also a form of anger.

The sages say anger is a type of idolatry. We forgot about the Holy One, we forget He's in charge, and give in to our anger. We blame the other person, whoever that might be. Blame is a kind of idolatry.

But, by talking to Hashem and asking Him to help us uncover our capacity for compassion and mercy, we are able to break our anger. Then Hashem mirrors us, and we merit Hashem's compassion and mercy. Even the harshest judgments against us can be diluted, softened and nullified when we break our cruelty.

May you have a day where you emulate God's Mercy and experience His unlimited Compassion.

26

Free Will

I n *Likutey Moharan* 151 Rebbe Nachman speaks about free will. In his prayer based on this teaching, Reb Noson says: "Filled with awe and wonder, how astounding is this power to exercise freedom of choice which you gave mankind, God. There is nothing as awesome and mysterious, as amazing and marvelous in all of the worlds which You made. Truly unique among your creations is free will."

Reb Noson explains that God gives his creatures the permission and the strength to make their own decisions and do what they will. We can choose to align with God's Will or the opposite, God forbid. Don't doubt that you too have been imbued with the ability and the strength to choose.

When we think about free will, though, we run into a wall because the existence of free will and God's foreknowledge is a paradox. If everything is determined by God, we ask, how come we are able to have free will? Why are we able to choose one thing or another? When we hit up against these paradoxes there is nothing that can bust through them except *emunah*. If we have *emunah* we understand that God created everything, including free will and including our limited intellect.

Don't try to understand this intellectually. Albert Einstein and Steven Dawkins wouldn't be able to make sense of this paradox. Even Moshe Rabbeinu couldn't understand this. A two-year old can't understand the theory of relativity and we can't understand the paradox of free will. That doesn't mean that it doesn't exist.

May you have a day where you live with emunah and make enlightened choices.

Remember the Truth

The essential truth of all of creation is actually quite simple. *All things were brought into being from nothingness by the Source, the One God.* At the end of time, when all of creation will be renewed, everything is destined to return to the Source.

But this isn't just an interesting philosophical debate. It matters in real life, too.

What happens when you fill your whole being with this truth at all times? What happens when you are aware and conscious that everything was created by God and everything will return to Him? Rebbe Nachman tells us that as a result of believing this, no falseness can ever have a hold on a person. What is falseness? Falseness is sadness, despair, anger, jealousy, and worry. All these things are rooted in falseness.

When you are able to remind yourself what the source of everything is, you can always return to that source, to the limitless shelter of God. There's a calming feeling in believing everything is ultimately headed to the pinnacle of purpose, that all of creation has a goal.

These beliefs and feelings can see us through some of our darkest, darkest times.

Once a friend of mine and her entire family experienced a shocking and tragic loss. A young family member died a violent death before he was married. He never experienced the joy of being a husband or parent, roles he had been so looking forward to. It was heartbreaking.

When I went over to comfort my friend she said, "I don't understand what happened, but I know that this must be good because *Hashem* only does good. I'm sad but I'm not giving in to despair." From the smallest child to the oldest great-grandparent, I didn't meet a member of that family who wasn't like a rock in *emunah*, even in the midst of their profound grief and pain.

That rock-like *emunah*, that belief that everything is from God, and that everything has an ultimate purpose, is what sustains this family, and what has sustained the Jewish people throughout history.

May you have a day where no falsehood can
ever encroach upon your peace of mind.

Getting What You Need

Rebbe Nachman tells us: *Pray for everything.*

If your clothing is torn and it needs to be replaced, pray to God for new clothing. If you need a new job or a raise, pray to God. Would you like to get through your errands quickly and easily? Pray to God. Do this for everything. Make it a habit to pray for all your needs large or small.

The Rebbe tells us that our main prayers should be about coming closer to the Holy One and growing spiritually. But he also tells us that we must also pray even for the little things, the material things. Hashem gives us food. He gives us clothing. He gives us a house or a place to live. Hashem gives us the basic things we need even if we don't ask for them. But, that's how an animal lives. God provides an animal with food and an animal doesn't have to thank Him or pray to Him or ask Him for more.

We are able to draw our lives down through prayer. We are able to talk to the Holy One. When we do, then we are truly human.

May you have a day where you remember that everything comes from God and a day in which you ask Him for at least one small thing you need or want.

29

Obstacles

There is a secret code-word among Breslovers. If you want to know if someone is a Breslover, mention the word *"meniot"*. This word means "obstacles". *Meniot* arise every day. Obstacles pop up to whatever it is you truly want to do. When Breslovers speak of *meniot*, they are usually speaking of obstacles that have something to do with spiritual growth.

Rebbe Nachman teaches that the greater the value of your goal, the bigger the *meniot* will be. But things are not what they seem. Obstacles aren't sent to stop you from fulfilling and achieving your goal, instead, they are sent in order to strengthen your desire to achieve your goal!

Want to get something important done? Know this: *The magnitude of the obstacles you will face is in direct proportion to the drive and desire you need to achieve something.* Rebbe Nachman explains that any time you want to do anything involving holiness, you are going to face obstacles. Do not let them stop you. They are there to specifically increase your desire. When you see an obstacle while you are engaged in doing something holy, like trying to come closer to Breslov teachings, rest assured that these *meniot* are a very good sign indeed.

> *May you have a day in which you remember the deeper purpose of every obstacle you encounter.*

Your True Potential

R ebbe Nachman said that a person should be careful not to let her smallness and sense of modesty overshadow her greatness and good qualities. In other words, a person will sometimes allow herself the luxury of thinking she is insignificant. Why is this a luxury? Because if she really indulges in this thought, she'll make no attempt to grow spiritually. She'll grow complacent. She'll think: *I'm nothing. I'm not so important.* Then, she'll feel no impetus to achieve the important things she was put on this earth to do.

This is a common affliction today. We live in a time when so many people don't actually believe in themselves. Each of us is a *chelek elokim*, a portion of the Holy One. We must remember: *Hashem* is great. Therefore, if we are a part of Him, we have greatness inside us, too. (Yes, we have the potential for bad, as well.)

The truth is: It's good to be modest. It's good to be humble. But it's not good to allow your humility or sense of modesty to overtake you and prevent you from doing the great things in life you were meant to do. You can accomplish. You just need to believe in yourself.

May you have a day where you recognize
your true, holiness-potential.

Emunah & Choice

Reb Noson tells us people can't know everything about their lives. No one can truly know what lies ahead. People can't get a clear handle on what they'll have to deal with. He says this ignorance is a good thing. It's vital to our identity, because the "not-knowing" is essential to freedom of choice.

Still, it's a trial for us, a test. It's frustrating. If you want to go through this trial and come out the other side, then you must have *emunah* in the Creator. You must also have faith in yourself. You have to believe that any movement you make towards a good decision, any step you take towards doing the right thing, is going to help you get through those hard times.

No matter what you're facing in life, if you truly understand that you don't have all the answers, yet you believe it's in your power to choose to do the right thing, you're going to be okay.

May you have a day in which your choices are clear.

Trust in Prayer

On the very last market day before Passover, Reb Noson still had no money to pay for the family's provisions for the holiday. As he was about to leave for the morning prayers, his wife stopped him and made it very clear that he needed to do something to get some money. She needed to prepare food for the Passover seder! Reb Noson said, "She taught me a chapter in depression this morning."

Even so he went to *shul* and prayed with no distractions. Afterwards, a fellow Breslover, Reb Nachman of Tulchin, saw a complete change in Reb Noson's face. All the worry was gone. It was clear he was filled with hope and joy, as if his prayers were already answered. A short while later some of Reb Noson's students and followers arrived in Breslov for the market day. They brought with them a huge amount of money which they gave to Reb Noson to use for Passover. It was enough to cover all the expenses for the entire holiday.

What was so remarkable about this was something more than just *davening* and getting what he asked for. Reb Nachman of Tulchin saw Reb Noson and said, "After he prayed, I noticed that his face had changed, he looked so calm. Later, I didn't see any change after he actually received the money."

The power of Reb Noson's *emunah* was evident. He was so certain that his prayers would be answered – it was as if he had already received the money in his pocket right after he prayed – that he didn't display extra happiness or relief when the money finally showed up.

Next time you pray think about your prayers and believe them to be already answered.

May you have a day of prayer and faith.

Bring Down the Wall

Somebody once came to Reb Noson and asked, "If all the tzaddikim of the previous generations with all their efforts couldn't succeed in bringing *Moshiach*, how will he come? With us, we're weak. We're not very pious. How can we usher in the era of redemption and peace on earth?"

Reb Noson answered with a story:

Once there was a very well-fortified city. It was surrounded by a very thick stone wall, which everyone said was invincible. One day a nearby king decided he was going to conquer the city. He looked at the fortifications and examined the wall and called together his top generals. He said, "Take your top troops, and the mightiest warriors in my kingdom, and attack the city. Bring down that wall. Conquer it." The soldiers tried and managed to make a slight scratch in the wall, but ultimately, they were defeated.

The king sent a second battalion of special forces to knock down the wall and conquer the city. They made a slight scratch in the wall, too. But they were also defeated.

Next, he sent all the soldiers that remained. These soldiers tried. They were defeated.

His entire army was destroyed but the king refused to give up. He once again rode close to the enemy city with his ministers. He examined the wall. He saw there were cracks in the wall. "The previous battalions achieved something important," said the king. "They made the wall weak so that even the weakest among us can take the city down."

The king knew what to do. He sent a few stragglers, some peasants and farmers and teenagers. They knocked down the already-weakened wall and conquered the city.

Reb Noson told his follower though the previous generations did not succeed in bringing the *Moshiach*, they did succeed in making cracks in the wall. Even though we may not be the elite, if we would make an effort, we could bring the wall down and usher in the era of *Moshiach,* worldwide peace on earth and redemption.

***May you have a day in which you believe
you can knock down walls.***

34

Ahavat Yisrael

I t can be difficult to truly love your friends. If your friend is more spiritually advanced than you, you might have a little resentment or even jealousy in your heart. If you are more advanced than your friend, then your friend might feel the same.

Rebbe Nachman encouraged us to hold on to the wish that our friends should be spiritually elevated. If only we could truly cultivate the desire that our friends grow spiritually, that they are close to God; if only we could be happy when they reach lofty spiritual levels – even if we ourselves can't reach those levels! If we can feel this way about our friends, this is a tremendous achievement.

We should do our best to think, says Rebbe Nachman, *Maybe I can't be a tzaddik but at least my friend should be one.*

Reb Noson tells us that he thought this was an obvious teaching. He was so pure and good, that he honestly rejoiced in his friends' success and happiness. But as he got older, he saw that many people became trapped by their jealousy. They felt they were unable to succeed spiritually so they provoked, discouraged and mocked those who were growing spiritually. They would even try to drag their friends down with them.

Rebbe Nachman tells us that if we truly love *Hashem*, we will do the complete opposite. And if we want to achieve some spiritual greatness (to the highest level that's possible for us, even if it's not as great as someone else's level), we will want to see our friends succeed. Your spiritual greatness may be acquired by being happy for someone else's spiritual greatness!

This is true Jewish love, Ahavas Yisroel.

> *May you have a day in which you love*
> *your friends and they love you.*

35

One Day

Rebbe Nachman found it very difficult to make *hitbodedut* when he was younger, even though he had a special room set aside for just this purpose. He felt it was impossible for him to open up and talk to *Hashem* with any depth. It went against his nature, his personality. However, he didn't give up. He forced himself to spend many hours in that room, speaking to *Hashem*.

This was true of everything in Rebbe Nachman's *Avodat Hashem*. Each act seemed to him like a tremendous burden. He remarked that it felt as if his spiritual service would actually crush him. Instead of giving up, though, he worked hard to find ways to serve *Hashem*. He would push himself to grow. He would tell himself, *I have only this one day. I'm going to ignore tomorrow and all future days. I have only this one day alone.*

In this way, by telling himself he only had to get through the present day, he ingrained in himself the spiritual habits that eventually made him a towering tzaddik. You can take a lesson from this on your own spiritual journey. If you're growth-oriented you know that just sitting and thinking about being spiritual isn't enough.

You need to pray. You need to do *mitzvot*. You need to learn a lot about the direction you should go in. You need to find a way to connect to *Hashem*. You need to learn authentic wisdom from authentic teachers.

In truth, this can seem overwhelming. But if you wake up and say, "I'm going to focus on today only. Here are the spiritual tasks I have set out for myself for today and that's all I need to focus on. I don't have to worry about tomorrow," this will help you stick to what you need to stick to. It doesn't matter how many spiritual tasks you have, or their variety. There might be a hundred in a day. There might be handful in a day. Wherever you're at, just remember that you only have to worry about one day at a time.

This isn't an empty, light promise. It really works. The Rebbe's followers use this technique to help them stay focused. It's far easier to put a lot of energy into one day then to put a lot of energy into this entire week, month or year.

May you have a day of focus and growth.

Pray Like A Child

R ebbe Nachman was very sick and close to leaving this world. His followers gathered around him, praying for his recovery. His grandson Yisroel came to visit and was ushered in. The little boy was only three or four years old.

The Rebbe said to Yisroel, "Pray to *Hashem* that I should become well again." His grandson sweetly asked, "Give me your watch and I'll pray for you." The Rebbe smiled and said, "You see, he's already a rebbe! He tells me to give him something in order to pray for me."

The Rebbe handed over his watch. Little Yisroel took it and said, "*Hashem, Hashem*, let my *zayde* be well again."

All the *Chasidim* laughed at the boy. But Rebbe Nachman corrected them. He said, "This is exactly how we have to ask *Hashem* for help."

In truth in what other way is there to pray to God? The essence of prayer is total simplicity, speaking to *Hashem* the way a child talks to his parent or the way a person talks to his very best friend.

May you have a day in which you pray like a child.

37

Constructive Criticism?

I n the last lesson Rebbe Nachman ever gave, he spoke about moral rebuke or correcting another person. It's true that there is a religious obligation (in many cases) to correct someone who is doing something detrimental to themselves or others. However, this is not always a good thing to do.

In fact, Rebbe Nachman said most people aren't capable of morally rebuking another person. The entire point of correcting someone is to inspire them to do better. Instead of achieving this, often they give chastisement and criticism that is harsh and painful for the listener to bear. What happens, says Rebbe Nachman, is that words of rebuke can stir up a bad smell, causing the stench of a person's failings to fill the air. Improper criticism also weakens a person instead of strengthening him. You might even push him further away from the right path.

Rebbe Nachman said only someone who is able to inspire and strengthen people, someone who is truly compassionate, is the kind of person who should offer moral rebuke.

What do we do in practical situations where we feel it is incumbent upon us to correct someone else? In most cases, this will involve a child. But a child is very, very sensitive. We must correct a child very delicately and carefully.

If it's an adult that you feel very close to, and you have the kind of relationship where you can be emotionally honest with each other, you might be able to offer suggestions in a gentle, positive way, maybe even indirectly. Again, if you choose to offer criticism, be extremely cautious that you don't hurt someone's feelings and that you don't alienate them or push them away. In most cases it's best to simply avoid correcting other people.

What if you are someone's mentor, and he comes to you for advice? Even then, tippy-toe around a little bit.

What about yourself? What about when you know that you need correction? You may realize you need moral guidance and maybe even rebuke. Yet even with yourself it's important to do it in a way where you don't tear yourself down. Make sure you are able to accept that you have flaws (like everyone else), and that this doesn't break you.

Most of the time it's simply better to focus on what you (and other people) are doing right!

May you have a day where you are able to point out the good in others and yourself.

38

Food's Healing Blessings

R ebbe Nachman teaches that *Hashem* can put the cure for what ails us into anything. Medicine can contain the healing energy we need. Air can contain the healing energy we need. Bread and water can contain the healing energy we need, too.

Before we eat, our sages tell us to make the appropriate blessing for the specific food we are about to consume. This blessing acts as a catalyst. It is a verbal formula which connects the energy in the food to its Source, Hashem. Also, this blessing thanks *Hashem* for being the source of the food, which heightens our personal awareness of where our food really comes from.

We take a bite, and if the food is kosher it contains spiritual molecules which have been activated by this blessing. We finish our snack or meal and say the appropriate after-blessing when we're done. This after-blessing unlocks healing energy which gets released as we digest the food. We've tapped into all this tremendous power by making blessings.

In addition to the blessings, in addition to the formulas and words, it's also important to have *emunah* and *bitachon* that only *Hashem* is the true source of healing. It's not the food itself. All healing comes from Him.

May you have a day where you believe in the power of the blessings you make.

39

Think Your Life

Does time appear to be flying by? Does your life seem to be fleeting? You wake up one day and realize the moments and hours have passed you by. You worry that the days and weeks are disappearing, too. Even a year (or a decade) doesn't feel like all that much time anymore. *How did this happen to me?* you ask. The answer isn't complicated. If we aren't finding meaning in life, the days blur together. If we are conscious of our spiritual goals and work towards them, our allotted time feels full, no matter how quickly it goes by.

Rebbe Nachman tells us that people almost never sit down and think about where they are headed, spiritually speaking. Most people spend more time thinking about what to eat for dinner than thinking about their soul. We make a lot of decisions every day. We Google and we read a lot, we certainly talk and text a lot. If we're highly motivated, we make pros and cons lists. But do we think about the really big decisions? Do we think about how our soul is doing?

Take some time in the early hours of the morning and take a walk, letting your thoughts keep you company. Or grab some time mid-day or very, very late at night when the world is quiet and still. Don't talk, don't read, just sit and think. Think about your spiritual future. Think about where you came from and where you are headed. Think about how you've grown and where you could improve.

We need to contemplate who we are and where we are going, says Rebbe Nachman. The time and place for this contemplation isn't as important as doing it regularly. If you're always rushing and you can't take a moment to internalize what you see and hear, if you can't find a moment to sit quietly and think about why you are here, why *Hashem* created you and put you in this world, then life will pass you by.

May you have day in which you seize every
moment and make them count.

The Power of Music

40

I t's common knowledge that listening to (or playing) music helps you experience either an amplification of, or a shift in, your mood. You know that music can make you feel sadder or happier, more social or more pensive.

Rebbe Nachman describes the power music has to totally transform a person. He says that when we hear music played on an instrument by someone who is a genuinely righteous person, and that person is playing with joy for the sake of heaven, this can be a catalyst to positive change. This type of music has the power to banish depression and bring joy.

This kind of holy music is also able to crush the power of the negative imagination. This imagination is fueled by the *klipot*, the primordial evil husks which contain negative energy leftover from Creation. During the month of *Adar* and the holiday of *Purim*, when we infuse our lives with joy, we banish this *klipa*-energy, which is embodied by *Haman* and *Amalek*. When we do, we are freed from apathy and doubt as well as from the self-destructive desires that overwhelm us. Even jealousy, anger, and other painful emotions are easier to let go of.

Music can do even more than this, says Rebbe Nachman. Listening to holy music can even help strengthen our memories – it's like ginseng for the *neshama*. This music, this holy music, helps us remember our unique purpose. Our soul connects with this kind of music. It sparks and glows from this kind of music. We become infused with new vitality that reminds us where we're headed and what we truly want out of life. We gain new insights when we listen to holy music. It can even help us attain a sliver of *ruach hakodesh*. It can help us connect to *Hashem*. Holy music can be the most powerful healing tool of all.

May you have a day in which you experience the joy of holy music.

True Greatness

Rebbe Nachman once told his followers that he didn't become a great tzaddik because of his great-grandfather, the Baal Shem Tov, or any of his other illustrious forebears. He became great because he worked on himself. In fact, he started when he was just a mere boy. He wanted so much to come close to God, and to gain a lot of *Torah* knowledge. He would force himself to talk to God all the time, even though this was difficult for him. He even gave his tutor his allowance money to teach him more *Torah*!

To develop spiritually, Rebbe Nachman first chose this as his goal. Then, he did everything possible to achieve his goal. Even though he often slid and fell, he always picked himself back up and started again.

He told his followers that they too, had the potential to become tzaddikim. If they would do as he did, choose their goal and stick to it through thick and thin, they could become great. If their chosen course of spiritual growth didn't go as planned and they fell down, well, they just had to pick themselves up and start again.

This message applies to you. It doesn't matter who your ancestors were. It doesn't matter who your parents were. It doesn't matter if you were raised in an ideal home, where everyone around you nurtured your soul, or not. It doesn't even matter who you were *up until this very moment in time.* You can make the decision that spiritual growth is your goal. You can make the decision that coming closer to *Hashem* is your goal. If you're serious, you won't be deterred from your goal, no matter what. Even if you slip and fall (and most everyone does occasionally), if you pick yourself back up and believe in yourself, you will achieve your spiritual potential in this lifetime.

*May you have a day in which you make good
decisions that move you forward.*

42

Find Joy in What You Do

Rebbe Nachman cautions us not to second guess our *mitzvot*. Once you've done a *mitzvah*, it isn't healthy to tear it apart and look for the flaws. That is not the way to improve. Rather, you should look for the good that you did. You should acknowledge it. You can even be proud of yourself if you're trying a *mitzvah* that is new or difficult for you.

For example, let's say you did the *mitzvah* of giving *tzedakah*. Don't say, "Wow, I really had to force myself to give. I'm probably very stingy. My heart wasn't in it. I know I could have given more." Stop this self-criticism. You gave charity! It's a good thing!

Another example is praying the daily prayers. Don't say "I really didn't concentrate and I didn't complete all my prayers. I kind of rushed through some sections. My heart wasn't in it."

You prayed! You talked to God!

Micro-scoping your *mitzvot* after the fact is self-defeating. Instead, emphasize joy. Yes, take joy and pleasure in the *mitzvot* you do. If, after you do a *mitzvah*, you nitpick the details and tear yourself apart, you diminish joy and exile yourself. You put yourself in the corner because you weren't perfect.

Of course, taking joy in the *mitzvot* you do doesn't mean that you don't need to spend some time each day figuring out where you need to improve. But Rebbe Nachman says that the majority of the day should be spent thinking positive thoughts about ourselves, other people, and *Hashem*. You should feel happy about what you're accomplishing and focus on what's good in your life. And, focus on what's good about you. The more you look for good, the more you'll find it.

May you have a day in which you find joy in the mitzvot.

43

Don't Be Embarrassed

Rebbe Nachman tells us that we should cultivate the trait of *azut d'kedusha*, holy boldness. One way to express this trait is by honestly telling a spiritual mentor about what's in your heart and on your mind. If you are fortunate enough to have a spiritual mentor, it's important to be able to speak without embarrassment. Just as you would with a therapist, express your questions and doubts. Ask your mentor how you can correct and fix the serious issues in your life, and what path you should head down in the future. If you're embarrassed, you won't be able to truly express yourself and you might miss out on important advice.

In the same way you should make *hitbodedut* with *azut d'kedusha*. Open up to *Hashem*. Tell Him your fears and worries, even the things you're ashamed of. Even though these feelings and words might be uncomfortable or painful, grab ahold of your inner strength and speak up. By doing this, you'll see that the answers will come your way. It may not happen right away, the very first time you speak to *Hashem* in *hitbodedut*. It may not happen the second or third time, either. But by opening up again and again, consistently, you'll see that the proper guidance will appear in your life. The answers will eventually come to you. If you keep at it, you will see an improvement, and you'll reach a place of inner peace.

May you have a day in which you are able to be open and honest with your Creator.

44

Questions about God

So, you have questions about God. You have questions about creation or why things are the way they are. You aren't alone. Rebbe Nachman says many people have serious questions about *Hashem*. These questions don't have to be ignored, but they can't necessarily be answered. The fact that they can't be answered reveals *Hashem's* greatness. If with our limited human intelligence, we were able to know everything there is to know about God, then we would be on the same level as the Creator of the universe. That would diminish His greatness.

You may have deep questions that aren't able to be answered in a way you can understand. If you do, our sages tell us that this is the point where knowledge ends and *emunah* takes over. Some people have a burning desire to know all there is to know. It takes a process of honest self-discovery for a person to realize that his intellect is limited. Just as an average person can't understand what a nuclear physicist knows about atomic nuclei and their interactions,

a human being can't possibly understand who *Hashem* is and how
He created the world.

> ***May you have a day in which you let***
> ***emunah take over when it needs to.***

How to Receive Compassion

The *Talmud* teaches that whoever shows mercy to God's creatures is himself showed mercy. In *Likutey Moharan* 119, Rebbe Nachman teaches that when you require *Hashem's* mercy and loving compassion, He is going to send you an opportunity to show your mercy and loving compassion to someone else. When you follow through by being merciful, you will have created a pipeline through which *Hashem* can pour his mercy and loving compassion down – onto you.

However, there is a secret ingredient you need in order for you to receive *Hashem's* mercy and compassion. That secret ingredient is *da'at*, holy awareness. At a simple level, if you have *da'at*, you are a person who is thinking about God a lot. You're not easily distracted from your true purpose in life. You don't get angry so easily. You're able to remember that *Hashem* is everywhere in this world (and beyond). You are someone who remembers that He is creating and sustaining this world at all times, and that everything comes from Him.

When you have *da'at*, you are also able to remember that the person who appears on your doorstep in need of mercy and loving compassion was sent to you by *Hashem*. This is probably going to trigger in you a very natural response to help, and to follow what the *Talmud* teaches. It says that whenever you show mercy, *Hashem* will show you mercy.

This can happen in an obvious and subtle way. For example, you might suffer for a long time from a minor ailment or complaint, or a difficult financial situation, or something along those lines. You may be offered opportunity after opportunity to help someone else with a situation that is causing them to suffer. If your response is "Leave me alone. I'm suffering. I can't help you, I'm not in a position to help you," you are wasting a precious opportunity for your own healing.

This is something that requires practice. You'll need "self-talk", in which you remind yourself what's really going on behind the scenes. Of course, what's really going on is every event, every conversation, and every person who crosses your path is sent to you from *Hashem*. They may be offering you a learning opportunity. They may be offering you an obstacle that you can overcome. They may be offering you a chance to share and receive *Hashem's* mercy and loving kindness.

May you have a day in which you feel compassion,
give compassion, and are given compassion.

Gently Stand Firm

H as this ever happened to you? Someone challenges you, confronts you or insults you because of your faith or your particular spiritual path within Judaism. Don't let it get to you – there is historical precedent. Throughout history Jews have been challenged for believing in Hashem and wanting to come close to Him. It's a fact of life.

These challenges aren't there to embarrass or humiliate us. They aren't there to turn us away from God. They are there so that we have the opportunity to strengthen ourselves and stand firm. If you believe in *Hashem* and the Jewish path, you might have been told that you are brainwashed or you must not be very intelligent. You might have been told you are living in another century and there is no need to be so sincere or extreme about your faith. You might be attacked openly by people who don't know you and even by people whom you are close to and love. Why? Because nothing pushes someone's buttons more than someone else serving *Hashem*.

This is the time to tap into your power of *azut d'kedusha*, which is holy boldness or holy *chutzpah*. Holy *chutzpah* will give you the ability to stand firm. But this is not the time to give into regular, old *chutzpah*, in-your-face brazenness. You might feel that you are right and that the other person needs to hear the truth, no matter what. But this merely escalates the conflict. It certainly doesn't resolve anything.

There really is no point in counterattacking or debating people who attack you about God, the *Torah*, and the true *Tzaddikim*, especially if they are people you care about. The best thing you can do is smile and stand firm. Say: "I allow you to be who you are. Allow me to be who I am." Then go live a good life. Be a better person. You never know. You might inspire someone else just by your actions.

May you have a day in which you are able to stand firm
while having true love and compassion for others.

47

Be Stubborn

Are you stubborn? Do people complain about your obstinacy? That's okay. Obstinacy can be a good quality, says Rebbe Nachman. In fact, he teaches that stubbornness is a requirement if you want to come close to *Hashem*.

When you yearn to come close to the Holy One, when you make a commitment to take that first step on your spiritual path, there is one thing you can be sure of: Obstacles will surely arise that will try and turn you away from your holy objective. Don't let them win. Be stubborn.

Continue to believe in *Hashem* and believe in yourself no matter what comes your way. Give yourself a pep talk. Give yourself encouragement. Don't listen to the naysayers or the people who say this path isn't for you. "What do you think you're doing?" they'll ask. "Who do you think you are to come close to *Hashem*?"

Don't pay them any attention at all. Only listen to your *neshama*. It's telling you that you come from a holy Source and you are connected to that Source. You can reach the greatest heights if only you believe in yourself. Don't worry about what other people say. Don't worry about what other people think. Believe and you will do. Believe that you are connected to *Hashem* and He wants you to walk towards Him.

May you have a day in which you are
stubborn for all the right reasons.

48

Rise to the Stars

The *Talmud* says that when the Jewish nation falls down, it falls down all the way to the ground. When it rises, it rises all the way to the stars. This isn't only true on the national level. It's true on the personal level as well.

Each of us has a potential to hit rock bottom, God forbid. We also have the potential to zoom through the stratosphere and rise to the highest heavens. It depends (in large part) on how we view ourselves and whether we have the *ratzon* to make the most of our lives.

At various times throughout the year we might hit a spiritual slump. We might fall down. Yet, from this low position we can rise up very high. We can use times of spiritual sluggishness for introspection, reflection, analysis, and *teshuva*. We can use these times to ask ourselves some tough questions:

"Will I remain content with the status quo? Or, do I truly want to grow spiritually?" Or as Rebbe Nachman asks, "Do you want to want?"

"Do I really understand what it means to be kind? Am I able to look for the good in myself and others?"

"Do I know what truth is and believe that truth is One? Am I honest about who I am and what I believe?"

"Do I yearn for *Hashem*? Do I long to come close to *Hashem* or do material desires get in the way?"

These tough questions are really not so tough. At the heart of each and every one of us, is holiness. There is a spark. There is a *nekuda tova*. Truly if you examine yourself very closely, you'll find that you yearn to rise to the stars.

May you have a day where your fall is small and your rise is great.

49

Victory or Truth?

Rebbe Nachman teaches that a person who wants to win all the time, who wants to dominate, who wants to be in the right, is a person who is actually unable to tolerate the truth. He says the truth can be staring that person in the face, but because he is determined to win at any cost, he is going to ignore the truth completely. If you want to find real truth in life, you have to rid yourself of the urge to win.

Sometimes we make a judgment about someone and we absolutely want to be right, so much so that we won't allow even an inkling of the truth to leak into our thoughts about this person. Sometimes we enter into an argument or disagreement. We want to win, just to win – no matter what the truth is. In our personal life, we may be unable to listen to the other person and hear what they are going through. They have a truth and we can't hear it. Sometimes at work or in business we want to dominate, we want to be victorious – even if it means we have to bend the truth.

Whatever the case may be, if we want to find the truth in life, we need to rid ourselves of the urge to win. Once we do, we will have clarity, we will see truth.

> *May you have a day in which the truth is dearer*
> *to you than your desire for victory.*

50

Three Prescriptions to Heal the Soul

Rebbe Nachman offers numerous prescriptions for psycho-spiritual healing. Here are three of my favorites:

First, be joyful. How? Make joy a choice. "I'll be happy when I win the lottery, get married, get that promotion..." No! Rebbe Nachman teaches that joy doesn't happen to a person. Joy must be a choice. It's something that one works to achieve. It is not something that comes from the outside. Until you try it, it will seem impossible to do. But our history is filled with ordinary people who achieved greatness by choosing joy in impossible situations. Nothing brings soul-healing like joy.

Second, embody wholehearted sincerity. Get rid of all the manipulating, scheming, planning, and overly-clever ideas that want to invade your thoughts. Live your life with your heart attached to the ones you love, and make sure those on your list include the Creator and the true Tzaddikim. Live straight. Live simple. The less you scheme the more you will love your life. The more you love your life, the more you heal.

Third, believe you can start over. Rebbe Nachman once said that he himself started over many times in his life, sometimes even many times per day. You must believe that nothing is irreparable. How? Imagine you're on a diet and a holiday like Shavuot comes along. You eat a little cheesecake and say, "Okay, I'll go back on my diet after the holiday." Then the holiday ends and you think "Well, the week is shot, it's already Tuesday, what's the point? I'll wait until next week to diet." This is an example of NOT starting over. This is an example of how to avoid starting over. When you start over, whether it's something material like a diet or something spiritual, make the choice to start over now. Keep it in the present. * Believe that whatever choices you've made in the past can be repaired. You are allowed to start over fresh.

Why is the idea of starting over so important? There is a Kabbalistic concept: the end is wedged into the beginning, and vice versa. The end can be nearly foretold from the beginning. If you want to build a house and you hire a great architect, but he doesn't build the foundation correctly, the house will collapse. The start was a failure.

Starting over allows you to correct things at the source, to go back to the root. This works for mistakes and transgressions, poor choices you've made in life, emotional states such as depression or anxiety, and other things you want to change. Believing you have the choice to start over is very, very powerful medicine.

May you have a day in which you remember you can start over.

---

* Many people are taught that there are transgressions that cannot be forgiven. Rebbe Nachman says this isn't true. Speak to a Breslov rabbi or mentor about how you can repair the past.

51

The Gift of Forgetting

When people go to see a therapist or a counselor, they often talk about the problems they faced in the past. Whether it is five, fifteen, or fifty years ago, they go over the past and look for new ways to make sense of the things that happened. They also dig deep in order to understand their own conscious and subconscious reactions. For many people, it's an important step to think about and talk through painful memories. This is all well and good – we all need to confide in people and discuss our lives.

But we also have to take the next step. That step is forgetting. In order to truly move forward, we must forget the hurt, the pain, the anguish. Rebbe Nachman explains that most people think of forgetting as a serious defect, but it is actually a very great gift. The past is gone forever and we don't need to bring it into our minds over and over again. If we can forget, we won't be disturbed by the past.

The Rebbe himself put this into practice in his own life. His way was to never go over finished business. Once he put it out of his mind, he never thought of it again. Why is this such a vital teaching? When we think of a traumatic or upsetting memory again and again, we actually rewire our brain to hold that memory. In essence, we have carved that memory into our brain. That manifests as an anxious, unhappy, fearful or angry feeling. Rebbe Nachman teaches that if we train ourselves to forget negative events, then we are free from them.

Our thoughts are our reality. Our thoughts and our feelings are deeply linked. Our feelings determine how we deal with every moment of our day. We react to the world around us with emotion. We want our feelings and emotions to be positive, but this must begin with our thoughts.

How can you forget? The Rebbe tells us to make a conscious decision to choose. If we choose to forget then we can literally harness the power of our minds to move forward (and not backward.)

May you have a day blessed with positive thoughts and memories.

52

Take A Running Jump

O ver two hundred years ago, in May of 1798, Rebbe Nachman left Ukraine and began his epic pilgrimage to the Land of Israel, which was then ruled by the Ottoman Empire. He traveled shortly after Napoleon's failed attempts to defeat the Turks in Jaffa and Akko. Not by accident, the Rebbe's travels occurred at the same time as the tumultuous beginnings of the Napoleonic Wars.

Along the way the Rebbe faced great opposition. He visited Constantinople (Istanbul), where he was in great spiritual and physical danger as he was mistaken for a spy. There, the Rebbe did something unusual. He took off his coat and hat. He took off his shoes, too. He then ran barefoot out into the streets and played for hours with the local children.

The games that he played with them were games of war, except he taught the children adult battle strategies. He would call one child France and another child another country. He would set up armies of children and they would all play out these battles. Some say the Rebbe was mystically arranging the outcome of the real-life battles through play, but we don't have a true understanding of how to interpret his actions.

On a simple level, the Rebbe was giving each of us a personal lesson. He was preparing himself to walk in the Holy Land and thereby attain the wisdom of the Land of Israel, a higher spiritual level. In order to do that he had to lower himself, make himself small. He ran barefoot and played games with children in the street, with no thought of his own dignity. Rebbe Nachman spoke of how his great-grandfather, the Baal Shem Tov, failed to reach the Holy Land because he couldn't make himself small enough.

Whenever a person is about to rise to the next level, he faces spiritual opposition which often manifests as material obstacles. The Rebbe wants us to emulate him. He teaches that he himself never remained at one level. We should not remain at one level, either. Throughout our lives we should also be growing and rising. But to go forward in life, we may need to take a step backwards. A period of lowliness, a period of complete simplicity or even childishness is often the prerequisite for spiritual growth.

Don't think if you go down you've regressed permanently. Think of it as a running jump. In order to take a leap, you back up, behind what you thought was the starting point. Then, you run. You get that momentum going and you fly!

May you have a day in which you embrace your own lowliness and believe this will propel you to the next level.

53

Azamra

ess than a month before Rebbe Nachman passed away, one
of his *Chasidim* asked him how one becomes great in *Torah*
wisdom. The Rebbe told him: *Never say a bad word about another
Jew.* When you blemish another Jew, in this case by speaking or
thinking ill of him, you are going to blemish and damage your
love for *Torah*. The reason is, the six hundred thousand letters in
the Torah are connected to the six hundred thousand root souls
of the Jewish people. They parallel one another.

The *Chasid* asked, well what do you do about the completely
wicked people?

Rebbe Nachman replied: *What? How can you say that about a Jew
that he is completely wicked? You must judge him favorably.* Then the
Rebbe exhorted this person to go out and learn and live *Azamra*.

Azamra is the foundational lesson in Breslov wisdom. Out of the
thousands and thousands of pages of Breslov learning that are
available to us, the few paragraphs that comprise *Azamra* are the key
to unlocking your soul rectification in this lifetime. However, Rebbe

Nachman and Reb Noson wouldn't have assiduously recommended we learn this lesson many times over, if it was so easily mastered.

When people hear *Azamra* they think, "Oh yes, that means I judge others favorably and then I judge myself favorably."

I've heard people say this and toss this concept off very casually. It's true that if you say it like that, it does sound like a poster from a school guidance counselor's office. However, *Azamra* is much, much deeper than this. It's not only about your relationship with other people and your relationship with Hashem. It's also about having a relationship with yourself. It's the first step towards understanding who you really are.

May you have a day in which you are
able to see the good in yourself.

54

The Creative Power of Thought

R ebbe Nachman says something remarkable. He says: *You must guard your thoughts carefully because your thoughts can literally create a living thing.* Thoughts, he teaches, are potent. He compares thoughts to other human faculties. You can throw something with your hand and it will go so far. You can call out to a person with your voice and it can travel even farther. A higher faculty is hearing because you can hear sounds like a cannon-shot, from very far away. Your sight reaches farther still. With sight, you can see the clouds, the moon, and the stars, all very far away. The higher the human faculty the farther it can reach.

Rabbi Nachman explains that the highest of our faculties is thought. Your thoughts are able to penetrate the loftiest heights, with them you can even think about the Creator. That's why you must cultivate awareness that your thoughts are very powerful and can literally create reality. In his lesson *Azamra,* Rebbe Nachman explains that when you find a drop of good in someone and judge them favorably you can actually change them from not deserving to meritorious.

Just by *thinking* kindly and favorably towards someone you help them change. How much more so does this apply to thinking kindly and favorably of yourself?

May you have a day where you pay attention to your thoughts.

55

The Song of Your Soul

A *zamra l'Elokai b'odee.* "I will sing to my God with the little bit I have left." These are the words from Psalms which give Rebbe Nachman's foundational teaching its name, *Azamra.* What do these words mean? In this little bit I have left, what is that? The little bit we have left inside is the *nekuda tova*, the good point inside each of us. That is the point that has no anger, depression, no jealousy, no sin. It's a pure shining radiant point of connection.

You have this point inside although you don't always feel like it. *Azamra*, I will sing, is the song of this point of goodness. It's the song of your soul. How do you sing the song of your soul?

When a person plays a musical instrument, she chooses a good note from a whole range of potential notes. She plucks out a note that sounds beautiful to her. Music is created from this choosing and separating, by selecting a good *ruach*, a good note, a good spiritual energy, and rejecting a negative spiritual energy. Negative energies are those of gloom, sadness, depression, despair, anger, and so on. When we identify and choose to focus on these good points, we create a beautiful melody. This melody is the song we compose and sing to our Creator.

Rebbe Nachman tells us it is impossible to pray if you are feeling depressed or bitter. How can you have a relationship with anyone including God if you feel bad about yourself? True, you may be able to cry out to Him about how much pain you're in, but you can't fully connect to Him in a way that brings you or Him pure joy. When you sing a beautiful song of your soul by focusing on the good points you have inside, you are creating a beautiful melody for *Hashem*, and for you and all of creation to hear.

May you have a day in which you sing the sweet song of your soul.

56

Wake Up

When a person feels distant from his Holy Source, he feels spiritually deficient and drained. When he feels numb, depressed or spiritually cut-off, this is called a state of sleep. The *Talmud* tells us that sleep is one sixtieth of death. Spiritual sleep is also a kind of death. How can we wake up? When a person starts to seek out the good point inside herself, when she looks at this point and becomes inspired by it, she feels joy. Then she begins to wake from her sleep.

King David says in Psalm 3:6, "I lay down and slept then awoke because God sustains me." How does God sustain a person? Reb Noson of Breslov tells us that the good point that we find inside ourselves is actually a point of Godliness. All good emanates from *Hashem*. When a good point exists inside us, this good is absolutely bound in unity with the Creator. We must understand that any good that exists, in whatever form it exists, is from *Hashem*. Any good inside us is therefore from *Hashem*, too. Therefore, He sustains each person. He sustains you, too.

When you look at that drop of Godliness inside yourself it can awaken you from your sleep and bring you back to joy. When you identify your *nekuda tova*,* it can bring you back to belief in yourself, in your self-worth. You'll truly understand that you have an important mission in this world and you need to be here.

May you have a day in which you remember that your life is a unique and vital part of creation.

---

* *If you aren't sure if you have a nekuda tova, just remember a mitzvah or some positive action that you did recently. This is an expression of your good point.*

Can You Live Happily Ever After?

When you were a child, you probably heard stories about little girls just like you who found out that they were secret princesses. They ended up marrying their prince, and living happily ever after. You hoped you would live happily ever after, too. Then you found out life is complicated.

Is it possible to live happily ever after? In *Azamra*, Rebbe Nachman tells us that when we choose to focus on and build up the good inside, we bring ourselves to joy. When we bring ourselves to joy, we connect with *Hashem*. When we connect to *Hashem*, we feel more joy.

There is more to it than that, of course. It's not just choosing the good, it's the process of choosing the good over the not so good. The actual act of searching, seeking, identifying and making that choice. The act of exercising our freewill is a workout for our happiness muscles. We strengthen ourselves in joy. We come to believe in ourselves. We come to believe that we can get up off the sofa and go chase after a *mitzvah* or do a kindness. We don't have to give in to despair, depression, laziness, negative thoughts or other self-defeating habits.

This isn't easy, but then, your life is not a fairy tale. Discovering your inner princess takes time. It takes training. It takes a commitment, just like going to the gym takes a commitment. If you can start to choose to develop the goodness inside and to live the goodness, happily ever after becomes a feeling inside.

> *May you have a day in which you believe you*
> *are able to choose to build your future self.*

58

What Type Am I?

This teaching of Rebbe Nachman's changed my life. Previously, I had been taught that there are three types of people. At the risk of oversimplification let's briefly lay them out: The *tzaddik*, a righteous person (a couple of types of *tzaddikim* exist.) Then the *beinoni*, the middle person. Finally, the *rasha*, a wicked person (a couple of types of *rasha* exist, too.)

I always found this idea confining, a little prison of predetermination. Why? Because I was taught that though there could be upward mobility from a *rasha* to a *beinoni*, it was generally not considered possible for the average person to become a *tzaddik*. I do not have pretensions of grandeur but when you're told you can only go so high or you'll bump your head on a ceiling, you don't push yourself to go any higher. Why would you? What would be the point?

Then I learned what Rebbe Nachman said. Rebbe Nachman used to get upset when anybody said that he achieved his spiritual greatness because his great-grandfather was the Baal Shem Tov. He said it had nothing whatsoever to do with his family. As a matter of fact, he proclaimed that spiritual success depends entirely on one's efforts. He told his followers that if they worked as hard as he had, they could also reach a very high spiritual level. They would become *tzaddikim*, too.

What do our spiritual achievements really depend on? Mainly our own free will. Now, perhaps the truth is that most of us won't reach dizzying spiritual heights. But when we look up and see that there really is no ceiling, we get the boost we need to try harder.

When you can say *I believe I can be a bit more spiritually advanced than I thought I could be*, you're partnering with God. You become a co-creator of your own life. You are choosing who you are. You are choosing where you're headed, many times each day, with every decision you make. When each of your decisions is nourished by the belief that you can achieve spiritual heights, you're lifted up to the next level.

May you have a day where you believe in your spiritual potential.

59

Got Advice?

Rebbe Nachman said that he was very positive about all the things he said and did. Because he really understood what he was doing at the deepest level, he had a calm certainty. He had reasons for everything he said and did. Still, he did not give his followers advice in the form of orders. Whenever the Rebbe gave advice he would suggest and recommend, he would gently guide. He wanted his followers to be free to follow his advice or not, as they chose.

Obviously, he wanted his followers to follow his advice because it was very carefully considered and wise, but he never insisted on anything. He had reasons for not insisting. He knew nothing in this world is perfect. Nothing in this world can possibly be perfectly good. Sometimes bad outcomes (at least in the short-term) can develop from good actions.

He also knew that there are always a lot of dynamics at play. Sometimes things go smoothly and sometimes not. People want to figure out what went wrong and want to blame someone. Rebbe Nachman didn't want to take that on.

He himself had this soft approach with almost everything, not just with giving advice. He never tried to force an issue. He never insisted that things should be exactly as he wished. He was always very flexible. He understood that there were many, many factors that affect everything that happens in this world.

How does this apply to us? One of the things we can take from this is that we all get asked for advice and we all give advice. You may give advice to your children, a relative, your friend, and so on. When you give advice, it may feel like your advice is one hundred percent correct. (After all, you're pretty smart.) Maybe you have well-developed insights; maybe it's true that the advice that you are giving is genuinely the right thing. However, what is also true is that the advice that you give might turn out topsy-turvy and upside-down. You can't possibly know everything. Therefore, it's important to let others know (and to understand yourself): There are no guarantees.

It's important to understand that we don't know everything. We shouldn't insist that things always be done our way. Sometimes we have to rule on the side of caution and say to others: "This is what I feel is the right thing to do. Based on my experience this is what seems right to me, however it's possible that I am not right. It's possible I am suggesting the wrong thing to you. It may not turn out well for you. Think about what I'm saying and consider it. Make your own decision. And of course, pray."

When it comes to ourselves, we also have to understand that we can't be stuck on the advice we give to ourselves. Sometimes we become rigid and insist on going only in one direction. The opposition we face may be really tough, even though we feel like we are doing the right thing. Maybe we're even trying to do an important *mitzvah*, but the opposition is so brutal, we can't do this *mitzvah* right now. Or maybe we are supposed to do it in a different way.

Sometimes we have to choose flexibility over accomplishment. How do we know if this is the time to make that choice? The first thing we can do is to talk to *Hashem* and ask for His guidance. *Hashem's* guidance is always perfect. We need to ask *Hashem* to set us on the right path. Talking to the Creator from the heart will help us clarify our correct path.

The second thing we can do is to learn what the true *tzaddik* teaches, and what all the great *tzaddikim* teach. We can follow their advice to the best of our ability and knowledge, resting assured that we are certainly aligning ourselves with *Hashem* and his *Torah*.

May you have a day in which you remember that sometimes being flexible is an important accomplishment.

Hermit Crab

A hermit crab lives in a borrowed shell. The shell is his home. At various times in his life he begins to outgrow his shell. He begins to feel the shell closing in on him. The shell starts restricting the movement of his limbs. It's not giving him room to breathe and grow. The hermit crab has to make a decision. He has to be brave. He has to decide to throw off the old shell. So, he shakes off his old shell in a moment of tremendous bravery and vulnerability. Then, he scurries across the ocean floor. He is exposed to all kinds of predators. He is exposed to all kinds of dangers while he hunts for a new shell. Eventually he finds a shinier, brighter, bigger shell.

When we are ready to get to that level of spiritual growth, it sometimes feels like our shells are closing in on us. Things are pressing us. Obstacles arise to meet us. We feel restricted and cramped. A person who isn't able to see *Hashem* in this situation might hunker down, curl up in a ball, and no matter how uncomfortable he is, he might stay in his old shell. A person with understanding knows that all this discomfort is a sign that now is the time when he is able to break through and reach that next level.

Rebbe Nachman tells us that no one is ever confronted with a barrier he can't break if he really wants to. Within the barrier, within the process of leaving that old shell, we find our new level. We find a new level of bravery, a new level of vulnerability, and a new level of possibilities for coming closer to *Hashem*.

May you have a day where you see opportunity in the obstacles.

Simple Spiritual Healing

ebbe Nachman's purpose in life was to spread spiritual healing. During his lifetime he gave his followers specific protocols to follow to achieve their personal *tikkunim*. One time he handed out a schedule of fasts, and one of his followers came up to him and said, "I'm very surprised at what you have given us. The fasts aren't many, and in fact there are very few. I would have thought that you would have given us many, many fasts so that we could be cleansed and healed spiritually."

Rebbe Nachman told him, "The problem with you is that you don't have faith that the simple things I tell you to do will actually help you heal."

Many kinds of obstacles can arise which can prevent us from completing our spiritual goals. Sometimes the obstacles are huge, but they come from the outside world. But the *yetzer hara* doesn't necessarily take the form of a missed plane, lack of money or a lack of connections. He doesn't always have claws and horns.

Most of the time the obstacle is internal – the *yetzer hara* inveigles our minds. There is a subtle, subtle kind of *yetzer hara* that's insidious and most convincing, and it will lead you astray. It will convince you that the prescriptions that the *tzaddik* gives you are just too simple. The Rebbe and other *tzaddikim* tell us: Say Psalms and you will find healing. But we can't believe that this is really going to help us. So, we become convinced that we shouldn't say Psalms or follow any other advice, at all.

Rebbe Nachman says: Start fresh and look at the world in new ways. Open your eyes and see that many of the spiritual tasks that are ahead of you are indeed simple, and even pleasant.

May you have a day in which you apply
the Tzaddik's simple advice.

More Spiritual Healing

When we try to follow the Rebbe's prescriptions, we often run into many obstacles. For example, we may try to say *tikkun haklali*, the ten Psalms, every day. Or we may try to practice *Azamra*, to look for the good in everyone, including ourselves. There are other easy tasks the Rebbe recommends. In actuality, these practices are genuinely simple. So why do we encounter so many obstacles that can make it difficult to do them?

The Rebbe explains that everything he prescribes is a helpful remedy for the past, the present, and the future – all of our existence, in fact. Therefore, while these remedies seem simple, they are also extremely valuable: they are treasures. Following his advice can have a profound effect not only upon each individual but also the entire world. That's also why, though they seem very simple, his prescriptions are very difficult to follow through on. The Rebbe himself said, "Everything I prescribe becomes very difficult."

When you try to carry out any of the Rebbe's wonderful remedies, just remind yourself that obstacles will arise. When you see an obstacle, pay it no mind. Ignore the obstacle and carry out the Rebbe's advice. Ultimately, it will lead you to deep spiritual healing.

May you have a day of spiritual healing and
following through on good advice.

How to Achieve Love and Peace in Prayer

The sages explain that as a result of feeling disconnected from other people and as a result of feeling that we don't really like (let alone love) each other, it becomes difficult for us to pray. Without love, words of true holiness aren't able to be spoken. True holiness always involves feelings of connection and love. That's why before praying we are told we should accept upon ourselves the positive *mitzvah*, "*v'ahavta l'reiacha kamocha*", love your neighbor as yourself. When we love our neighbor, we bring forth love and peace. The kind of speech we need to speak during words of prayer also emanates from love and peace. Love and peace are where the source of true prayer lies.

The truth is, it can be very difficult to honestly love and feel peaceful towards others.* Especially difficult to love are those people who challenge you, who push your buttons, who maybe even insult you or worse, God forbid.

---

*Remember: *Hashem* doesn't give us any task that we are unable to accomplish.

What should you do? Look for the good in those people! Identify the good they surely must have somewhere inside and focus on that. Clear your heart of disdain or dislike before you pray. Sincerely and honestly clear your heart. When you do, your prayers will go to the next level.

Rebbe Nachman teaches this in *Likutey Moharan*, but of course this is a universal Jewish teaching, the importance of which can't be overestimated. Connecting with people, making friends, keeping friends. Looking at people who maybe aren't close friends – maybe they're not your cup of tea – and making sure you find the good about them. Certainly, don't look for the bad things about them. Try and dissolve any grudge you might have in your heart against anyone. *In this way all your prayers will be heard.*

You can clear your heart of dislike before the daytime prayers. Do it too, before you say the prayers at night. Ask God to help you not hold a grudge against anyone. Pray that no one be punished on your account.

May you have a day in which you believe you can love others.

Speech is A Mother of Children

R ebbe Nachman tells us that speech is "a mother of children." Why? A mother always stays with her child. She always keeps her child in her heart. She never forgets her child even if she goes to the lowest of places. So too, the power of speech never leaves a person. Even if she finds herself in a low place, a place of depression, frustration, anger, or other spiritual danger, speech remains.

Even if you are sunk in a such a place, you can always remind yourself of Hashem's presence as long as you speak. Speak words of holiness, words of *Torah*, words of prayer, words of kindness. Read some Psalms aloud. Talk about God to yourself, your friends, your family and neighbors.

When we use our speech to talk about positive and holy topics, we are always able to remind ourselves that Hashem is near. His presence is with us no matter how far we may think we are from Him. Rebbe Nachman tells us that speech won't desert you. It won't desert you if you don't desert speech! He explains that the tremendous power of speech can save you from spiritual destruction. Think before you open your mouth. Think before you click. (Writing is also a kind of speech.) Think before you hit send. Take a moment and ask yourself: Are these words of kindness that I would want written in the *Torah* of my life?

> ***May you have a day where you speak
> and hear kind and true words.***

Hitbodedut

itbodedut, sometimes translated as personal prayer, often comes with a set of instructions. You might hear from someone that you should use a particular formula when making *hitbodedut*. One formula begins with praise of and thanks to Hashem, and moves on to heartfelt confession and remorse for transgressing, followed by requests. There are other formulas, too. Actually, Rebbe Nachman did offer advice about how to have personal conversations with Hashem. Sometimes he did suggest specific formats.

However, Rebbe Nachman also said *hitbodedut* is about offering yourself up to Hashem. It's about expressing your innermost thoughts and feelings to Hashem. Confiding in Him just as you would confide in your very best friend. This really is the essence of *hitbodedut*.

It's important to understand that if you are struggling to get started, you don't need to make *hitbodedut* complicated. Sure, try formulas. But, if you do and they aren't working for you, don't worry – just keep talking to your Creator. The main thing is to talk (out loud or at least in an audible whisper), because that is how we build relationships. This is especially true for women. Women talk and through conversation we get to know each other. The reason to talk is to make connections, even if we are talking about everyday topics. We share ourselves with someone else and they share themselves with us. We have a relationship.

Just as a mother babbles silly rhymes to her baby or a couple says sweet silly things to each other, we build relationships through even the simplest forms of speech. When we speak more eloquently to each other (and listen), we develop sympatico. We connect to another's rhythms and sensibilities. This is similar to what happens with our relationship with Hashem.

Reb Noson tells us something astonishing. Maybe you're not so articulate. Maybe you have intense feelings but are unable to express them in words. *It doesn't matter.* When you truly yearn to open up to Hashem, you will find that Hashem Himself will place words in your mouth. He will give you the words to speak to Him. Then you'll be able to offer up a beautiful prayer. A beautiful prayer composed of beautiful words is truth.

Your deepest truths, layer upon layer of truths, are the heart of your connection to Hashem.

*May you have a day where you are able to
express the words in your heart.*

Emunah vs. Envy

Some people believe that the world's resources are finite and that life is a zero-sum game. They believe that only they themselves truly understand how to divide up the food and money, the power and prestige, and the wisdom and knowledge, in the right way. They think that if someone else divides it up, somebody somewhere is going to do without. Of course, many of the ideologies that sought to distribute and divide up all the world's resources led to some of the greatest mass murderers and death by starvation the world has ever seen.

We have a different understanding. We understand that Hashem created and sustains the world. We believe that where the resources go are determined by Him. This is why the emotion of envy is in conflict with a genuine belief in Hashem. If we see that someone has something particular (a beautiful house, a prestigious job, honor and status, money, a beautiful family, a trophy spouse, and so on and so forth), and we are going crazy with envy because we want what they have, we are in effect saying that Hashem didn't divide the world's resources up fairly. It's like saying, "I don't think that the Creator of the Universe got it right."

There is an even more insidious kind of envy. It is based on an even greater lack of *emunah* than wanting what someone else has. That is the kind of envy and jealousy that says, "I don't want what the other person has, I just don't want her to have it." This kind of envy comes from a lot of confusion, pain, and hatred.

Rebbe Nachman speaks a lot about jealousy and envy throughout his teachings. He does this because first of all, these are very human traits and we have to acknowledge this. Second of all, the good news is that jealousy and envy are traits we can identify, work on and actually get rid of. Once we understand that feeling jealous or envious shows a profound lack of belief in Hashem's ability to run the world in the best possible way, we take a solid step forward on the path towards *emunah*. And with stronger *emunah*, we gain freedom from all kinds of covetousness.

In the *Aleph Bet* book Rebbe Nachman says something incredible. He says that when envy is eliminated it's going to herald the ingathering of the Jews from exile. It's going to usher in the *Geula* and the era of *Moshiach*. Why is that? Why envy in particular? The era of *Moshiach* is an era of *emunah*. Thus, the entire world will be filled with faith.

In order to begin to get to that stage we can't be envious or jealous of each other. We must cultivate the ability to look at another person and rejoice with them over what they have, even if we don't have it. We must be happy for them even if they have a greater measure of spirituality or *Torah* knowledge than we have. As a matter of fact, this is real Jewish love. The Rebbe tells us to be happy for another person even if spiritually they are greater than us.

May you have a day where you are happy
for others and content with your lot.

Stories

R ebbe Nachman famously said, "Other people tell stories to put people to sleep. I tell stories to wake people up."

He explains that when a doctor is healing a blind person it is necessary to put him in a darkened room with diminished light, and to let the light in little by little. This way, the light will not harm him when he suddenly sees. Similarly, when someone has been spiritually asleep in the dark for a very long time, the healer must use caution and make sure the spiritually blind person doesn't suddenly become overwhelmed with spiritual light.

Rebbe Nachman has a way to diffuse the light. He gently begins to help people to see, to softly wake them up. The method he uses is the telling of his famous stories, the tales of ancient times. Rebbe Nachman has many stories but there are thirteen main tales, each containing very powerful medicine. The first tale is called "The Lost Princess". It contains deep secrets which are cloaked in a simple and interesting story. It is about a king who banishes his daughter, the princess, from the castle. The king's viceroy, his faithful servant, goes on a long journey to find the lost princess.

The important thing about the Rebbe's stories is to read them (preferably out loud) in whatever language you are comfortable. It is good to have some understanding of the deeper meaning of the tales. Even though Reb Noson offers rich commentary on the tales, we don't have access to all the meanings because they are so very deep. But we do know, for example, that the king at the beginning of this story (and other stories) is *Hashem*. The lost princess is the *Shechina*, *Hashem's* indwelling presence. And the lost princess can also be the *neshama*, the beautiful soul inside each of us. The viceroy is each one of us. The viceroy's job is to search out and find the lost princess and bring her out of exile. We are here to take our soul (and the soul's we are connected to) out of exile.

You can start by reading the Rebbe's stories out loud to yourself, your family, and friends. You can begin the task of rescuing your own lost princess, taking her out of exile and freeing her.

***May you have a day in which you begin
to find the story of your life.***

The Very Narrow Bridge

The famous song, *Kol Haolam Kulo*, is based on a line from *Likutey Moharan* II, 48, "Know! A person must cross a very narrow bridge, the main thing is do not let yourself become frightened at all."

We know that our life is the crossing of a narrow bridge. In fact, every day we cross many bridges. We have to hang on tight. It feels like our fear comes from the outside, from the situations we face in life, from the external bridges. But in actuality all fear comes from the inside. That's why the language in Rebbe Nachman's famous teaching implies that fear is something that we cause ourselves.

Much of our worry comes from a lack of knowledge about what is going to happen next. Rebbe Nachman is telling us what we need to do. We need to put one foot in front of the other and concentrate on the present, so we don't slip and fall off the bridge.

My husband works with youth and adults who are dealing with a range of emotional health problems and addictions. Every week it seems that somebody comes into the clinic and talks about committing suicide. Once a boy in his early twenties came. It seemed like everything was going wrong for him. He had built a business. It collapsed. His girl left him. He was dealing with an addiction to painkillers. He came into the clinic and said, "I want out. I don't want to be in this world anymore." In other words, he wanted to jump off the bridge.

My husband sat down with him and talked about Rebbe Nachman. He let him know that each and every one of us is crossing a narrow bridge. It may feel that what we're going through is unique to us, and in some way, it's true, it is unique. But we all have fears. We all have loss. We all have worry. We all have times when we feel that the negative things that we are going through are more intense than anybody else's negative things. Really, they are not.

The next thing to remember is that Rebbe Nachman says we are able to begin again, any time we want. We are able to start over. We have to start over. We begin by putting one foot in front of the other. We must understand that anyone who does make it to the other side, which thank God is most of us, it's because they simply put one foot in front of the other. They didn't look down into the canyon under the bridge. They kept their eye on the next step, and the ultimate goal.

May you have a day in which you take one step at a time.

Your Main Weapon

The Messiah's main weapon is prayer. Now, *Moshiach* has other weapons too. *Torah* and *mitzvot*, humility, righteousness, and more. Still, his main weapon is prayer. Rebbe Nachman tells us that this is how *Moshiach* is going to conquer the world. He will bring each person to the awareness that prayer (opening our hearts and mouths to the Creator) is the source of our spiritual and material sustenance.

Rebbe Nachman also tells us that every person has a little bit of *Moshiach* inside him. Therefore, each of our personal main weapons is prayer. But what happens when we go to speak to Hashem in prayer and we can't open our mouths? Or we are not able to speak from the heart?

Each person has burdens weighing them down, both spiritual and material burdens. We have a body and its desires and needs weigh us down, too. We have a tiny, niggling (or not-so-tiny) doubt that maybe opening our mouth in prayer isn't really the answer. What do we do?

Rebbe Nachman tells us that no matter if even all the above is true, pay it no mind. Grab ahold of yourself with all your strength, and force yourself to cry out to Hashem. Pull your voice out from your heart with as much truth as you can muster. If you keep doing this, over time, you will find that you will generate an expansive awareness in which you really feel connected to Hashem at all times. You will be ready for *Moshiach*.

***May you have a day in which speaking
to Hashem comes easily to you.***

Be A Person of Truth

Rebbe Nachman tells us that the truth is one and the source of truth is oneness. Falsehood is sourced in multiplicity and division. There can only be one truth. Grabbing hold of that truth and hanging on tight will lead you to the ultimate Source of everything: Hashem. How can you become a person of truth? Start by not being dependent on other people for their admiration. Rebbe Nachman tells us that when we are dependent on others for honor, praise and so on, we won't be able to be truthful. All our gestures, words and behaviors will be used to elicit a positive response from others. We'll lose our capacity to express ourselves with genuine gestures, authentic behaviors and straight words.

We will also end up fooling ourselves on the inside. The Rebbe explains that if we're busy trying to impress others, we'll become bogged down in rationalizations. We'll tell ourselves stories to explain to ourselves why we are behaving in certain ways. "Oh, it's not that I want to see my name in lights, it's not that I want other people to look up to me…but instead the story will be: "I'm doing what I'm doing because I'm extra pious and spiritually advanced."

If we worry about impressing others, we will end up losing track of our own motivations and we'll lose track of our true self, too.

When we live in truth and oneness, however, we don't draw our sustenance from anything but Hashem. We live authentically. We live life as a free person without the burden of having to impress someone. When we live in truth it feels like having a slice of heaven on earth. As a matter of fact, Rebbe Nachman explains living free like this is akin to bringing the redemption in our time. When *Moshiach* comes and the world is at peace, we are going to be so busy praising Hashem and loving one another, we aren't going to be concerned with adoration, flattery, and compliments. We will simply want to connect to Hashem in truth.

May you have a day of being real.

Making Things Right

R ebbe Nachman says "If you believe you can damage, then believe you can repair."

When we make an error, when we transgress, our defense mechanisms can kick in. We might go into denial. We might project the blame out onto others. We might pretend it never happened. Or, we feel sad and despondent that it did happen. We beat ourselves up. *None of this solves the problem.*

What solves the problem is turning to Hashem. Turn and return to Him and believe that He loves you so much that He wants you to come back to Him. Believe He is going to help you heal the misstep or transgression.

We are told that when Hashem accepts our *teshuva* (which he will do – which he *yearns* to do), He turns our sins into merits. What we need in order to get back to Him is the belief that we are capable of getting back to Him. We also need to believe and know that Hashem loves us so much that He is waiting for us to return.

May you have a day where you believe that Hashem loves you and wants you, and you believe in your own ability to come back to Him.

Today Could Be Your Birthday

When we are asleep, time does strange things. Reb Noson gives an example. We may take a nap for only fifteen minutes but during that brief time we can have a dream in which seventy years have passed. When we wake up, of course we know that only fifteen minutes have gone by. What is going on?

When we are asleep, we have restricted consciousness. We have limited awareness and understanding. Sometimes, people live their entire lives as if asleep. They live with restricted consciousness. Then, their understanding and experience of time can be just as illusory as a dream.

Reb Noson tells us that there is a realm beyond time. When we put our hope in Hashem who is beyond time, we have eternal hope. When we hope for the World to Come, we find a remedy for all the days and years we wasted. The truth is that our only hope to make things right lies in the realm beyond time. This truth is the source for all soul healing.

If you buy into the illusion that time controls you, that you are time bound, limited and that nothing exists in this world but time, then you are stuck. If you have faith in Hashem, you know and believe that Hashem is in a realm beyond time. In fact, He created time. If you don't tie yourself up in time's straitjacket, it's like being born today. Then every day is your birthday.

May you have a day of expanded consciousness and a fresh outlook.

73

Quiet Miracles

During the Rebbe's lifetime, one of his followers came to visit him for *Shabbat*. His arm was in a sling and he had been unable to move it for some time. Also, the man was very poor and he couldn't afford the treatments necessary to begin the healing process. As they were sitting around at the Shabbat morning meal, the Rebbe turned to his followers and asked, "Doesn't this man have a lot of faith?"

His followers looked at this man whose arm was in a sling and they said, "Yes, he does."

The Rebbe asked a second time, "Doesn't this man have a lot of *emunah*?" Again, they agreed.

All of a sudden, the Rebbe said to the man, "Lower your arm." And, he did!

All the men were shocked. They sat around the table open-mouthed. The man had arrived unable to move his arm. Just as suddenly, the man listened to the Rebbe and was able to move his arm. His arm was healed. It is said he remained healthy for the rest of his life.

The Rebbe's miracles were rarely publicized, although we know he made many, many miracles. During his lifetime the Rebbe minimized his involvement in miracles because of the spiritual cost of doing miracles. In fact, he asked people to forget about the miracles he performed.

The Rebbe also wanted us to understand that we don't necessarily go to him for an overt miracle. Sure, we do want miracles. We do want things in our life to change. But there is something more valuable we can attain than an obvious miracle. We go to the Rebbe to find a different type of miracle, the miracle of soul-healing and personal growth. An inner miracle.

When we come close to Rebbe Nachman and study his teachings*, we change. We grow. We begin to see quiet miracles in the midst of our ordinary lives. And sometimes we are blessed to see more of the noisy miracles, too. We grow and we come closer to Hashem; we learn a lot about ourselves and our mission in this lifetime. This is the greatest healing and the greatest miracle of all.

May you have a day of revealed blessings and miracles.

*Traveling to Rebbe Nachman's gravesite in Uman, Ukraine can be a powerful catalyst, too.

The Truest Truth

Sometimes what looks like the best possible situation may cause us to lose our way, spiritually speaking. We need to remember to ask ourselves whether or not an opportunity or offer is going to be conducive to our spiritual growth and service of God.

Once Reb Noson was offered the job of chief rabbi in a nearby region of Ukraine. His father-in-law was pressuring him to take the job because it was a prominent position and would give him not only prestige, but also a very good income. But Reb Noson's heart wasn't in it.

Now, Reb Noson's main goal in life was serving God. And he wasn't sure if this job would help him meet his goal or if it would be a distraction. He just wasn't sure what to do. So, he went to Rebbe Nachman for advice.

"Should I take the job," he asked?

"Why not", said Rebbe Nachman, "Being a chief rabbi is a pretty big deal."

Reb Noson was always respectful of the Rebbe, but he wasn't satisfied with the Rebbe's answer. He asked him, "Is that the true answer? Is taking the position of chief rabbi the correct thing to do?"

Rebbe Nachman said again, "Why not?"

Reb Noson was still unsettled. He felt that he needed more. He asked the Rebbe, "Is what you're telling me the *emeser emes*, the truest truth? Is it the real truth?"

"You want the *emeser emes*? The *emeser emes* is that you should definitely *not* take the job of chief rabbi." Reb Noson went back home and told his family he was no longer considering accepting the position.

Later in life Reb Noson would speak about this. He would fervently rejoice and thank God that he had followed the Rebbe's advice. Reb Noson knew that his whole life he was able to serve God in the truest way possible because he wasn't worried about honor or prestige or making a lot of money. For him, this was like winning the lottery of life. This brought him tremendous joy.

May you have a day where you connect
to God with the emeser emes.

Obstacles are Gifts from God

During World War I there was an affluent and educated town in Ukraine near Uman, where Rebbe Nachman is buried. The inhabitants of this town noticed discrepancies and contradictions in their religious books. Their religious leaders couldn't answer their questions so they turned to the Jews.

They saw that the *Torah* made sense and so the people of the town decided to convert to Judaism. Because of the backlash against Judaism in general, and Jewish conversions specifically, it was hard for them to find people who would help them convert.*

Some Breslover *Chasidim* were brave enough to assist them. They remained close to the converts and gave them tremendous support throughout their lives.

Why would God make it so hard for someone to come closer to Him and His Torah?

---

*Helping a non-Jew convert to Judaism was dangerous, and the person helping the non-Jew risked his life.

When someone who is far away from Hashem wants to come closer, he faces tremendous obstacles and opposition. Family members and friends may get angry or upset. Money issues and other confounding issues may arise. Fears, anxiety, and worry may become part of what he has to deal with every day.

Any person who wants to come closer to Hashem must know and believe: The obstacles that arise are actually sent to you from Hashem (just as everything in your life is sent from Hashem.) Within the obstacles themselves, not only will you find new knowledge and new ways of understanding yourself and your relationship with God, but you will find God Himself. He is in the obstacles. The obstacles are there to increase your desire to come closer to holiness.

Don't give up! Just because you must struggle, just because people oppose you or you don't get what you pray for, if you genuinely want to come closer to Hashem, don't stop turning towards Him.

May you have a day in which you find the
holiness hidden in the obstacles.

Five Channels of Wisdom, Insight and Holy Awareness

F ive times in the history of creation the pure path of truth was renewed and revealed. First, through Moshe our teacher, who brought down the Written Torah and the Oral Law from Mount Sinai. Next, through the second century, C.E. sage, Rabbi Shimon Bar Yochai, renowned student of Rabbi Akiva and the author of the *Zohar Hakadosh*. He was able to reveal the highest level of esoteric truth possible in his time.

After him, in the 1500s, came the holy *Arizal*, Rabbi Yitzchak Luria, who had the ability to pass down entirely original teachings to and through his students. These teachings sustained the world until the coming of the next in this chain, the Baal Shem Tov. The Baal Shem Tov revealed remarkable mystic and moral teachings that sweetened the confused suffering prevalent in his time.

Then the Baal Shem Tov's great grandson, Rebbe Nachman, came along. He brought out into the open totally awesome, exalted and utterly unique teachings. He taught that his fire would burn until the coming of *Moshiach*. We can count on the fact that Rebbe Nachman's teachings are unparalleled, and are in fact the *Torah* of

Moshiach. They prepare us for the redemption, the coming period when the world will reach its highest purpose and there will be peace on earth.

How does learning these teachings prepare us?

When we attach ourselves to Rebbe Nachman and his teachings, when we follow his advice and his guidance, a spark of the light of holiness is drawn down into us, each person according to his level. It doesn't matter who you are: when you genuinely learn the teachings of the *Tzaddik Emet,* you will start to yearn for truth. You'll want something more out of life and you'll want to know what the meaning of your life is. You will learn that God is calling you and that you are very, very precious to Him.

Rebbe Nachman helps us to understand that each person, including you, is dear to Hashem. You are His beloved. This world He created would be a poorer place without you. You are essential to the story of everything. In fact, your unique life is integrally woven into the fabric of Creation. Once you understand that everything in your life is actually about coming closer to Hashem, once you start putting Rebbe Nachman's advice into practice, you'll begin to discover who you truly are, that is, a very holy being with lofty potential. You will live a life of meaning and joy.

May you have a day in which you learn the
teachings of the true Tzaddikim.

Find Yourself in Prayer

Rebbe Nachman teaches us that we should try to find ourselves in all the prayers composed by our sages, especially Psalms. If we read the prayers out loud, without sophistication, and with openness and joy, we will begin to find ourselves. When we pay attention to the simple meaning of the words, we will see ourselves within the prayers. This is especially true of *Tehillim*, the beautiful Psalms which were composed on behalf of the Jewish people by King David.* (And even more, know they were written on behalf of you personally.)

Rebbe Nachman teaches that the main thing is to talk to the Creator, using the words of the sages as well as our own words. In truth, we should be talking to God all the time. This will transport us from darkness into the light.

Sometimes we get discouraged. We feel like we've been crying out to God for a very long time. We still feel disconnected. We still feel unheard. Why does this occur?

* Everyone is encouraged to say Psalms.

Hashem determines the exact amount of prayers that a person needs to say in order to get that click. Rebbe Nachman assures us that if you keep on talking to *Hashem*, using the words of King David as well as your own personal words from the heart, *Hashem* will answer you. For some people this might take a few days or weeks. For others, it can take a lot longer. But if you remain strong and you remain brave, and strengthen your faith that your prayers will have an effect, they will.

Emunah is like any other muscle. It has to be exercised. Big, strong *emunah* muscles aren't something that you are just automatically given. You've got to train them. Don't give up on praying too quickly – it takes time to get stronger. When you speak to God in truth, you strengthen your faith. When you strengthen your faith, it brings you closer to God. Eventually He is going to accept your prayers and you are going to have the sweetest of feelings – that you are very close to Him. You will discover yourself in this relationship.

***May you have a day in which you believe
in the power of your prayers.***

Sitting with The King on His Throne

R ebbe Nachman tells a short story. A king once went hunting. He traveled in ordinary clothing like a simple man, so that he would have freedom of movement. Suddenly a heavy rain fell. It was a deluge. In the confusion, his ministers forgot about him and scattered in all directions. The king was in great danger from the flood. He was all alone. He searched the forest until he found the cottage of a peasant. The peasant invited the king in and offered him some kasha. He lit the stove and led the king to a pallet on the floor to sleep. This was very sweet for the king. He was so tired and exhausted it seemed as if he had never before had such a pleasurable experience.

The next morning the rain stopped. The royal ministers went out to search for the king. They finally found him inside the peasant's cottage. They wanted him to return to the palace with them. "You did not even attempt to rescue me," said the king. "Each one of you ran to save himself. This simple man rescued me. Here I had the sweetest experience. Therefore, he is the one who will bring me home, in his wagon, in my tattered clothes. He will sit with me on my throne."

Rebbe Nachman said that in the times before *Moshiach* comes, there will be a flood of atheism and immorality. This flood will cover all the high mountains, even the mountains in the Holy Land where the original flood did not reach. This time it will come with such strength that the waters will splash over all the land. The flood will have an effect on even good and pure hearts. Rebbe Nachman says there is no way we can combat this flood with sophistication.

Today, all the world's ministers have scattered. They're looking after themselves, running for their lives. The only ones who are able to battle this flood are the simple people, those who recite Psalms with faith. This is why simplicity is the key to faith and the key to the Redemption. Simple people will be the ones sitting with the King on His Throne.

May you have a day of simple faith.

You're the Director of Payroll

The Breslov teacher Rabbi Eliyahu Chaim Rosen told a story about the Maggid of Mezritch, who led the nascent Chassidic movement after the Baal Shem Tov's passing. A wealthy man came to the Maggid and announced that he had taken upon himself to fast and mortify his body. The Maggid wasn't pleased. He grabbed him by his lapels and said, "You are not allowed to fast. You must feast on fish and meat every single day!"

Chastened, the rich man left. The Maggid's students asked why he had instructed the rich man to feast every day. Would it be so terrible if this man denied himself some pleasures of the body? The Maggid explained. If the rich man himself eats fish and meat, he'll maybe understand that the poor need to get at least the basics like bread and milk. But if he himself only eats a crust of hard bread, what will be left for the poor?

We're taught that the wealth that we have is really God's money. He gives it to us so that we can spend it on *mitzvot* and so that we can give *tzedakah*. Our job is to personally distribute the money in our keep fairly, according to the teachings of the sages.

However, there are some who believe that the money in their hands is their own and that they earned it. They do not accept that it has come to them through *Hashem's* blessings. These people find it difficult to understand that they are conduits for *tzedakah*.

There is a spiritual rule about *tzedakah*. When we give what we are supposed to give and even beyond, we correct the pipelines of blessings and abundance that come down onto us and onto the world at large. By channeling this abundance to a poor person* we channel it to ourselves.

May you have a day in which you have an abundance of blessings.

*Poverty may be material or spiritual (or both.)

80

The Art and Science of Joy

The *Talmud* teaches that for the merit of even one *tzaddik*, the world was created. Why? What is the role of the *tzaddik*?

An important quality of the *tzaddik* is his ability to bridge the spiritual and material worlds. One of the ways in which he does this is by teaching us ordinary people, those whose lives are rooted in material existence, that there is a spiritual reality underlying and informing every aspect of our lives. A vital step in our spiritual growth is gaining the ability to recognize this and to become truly aware that the Creator is constantly sustaining us.

The reason why we learn the *tzaddik's* teachings is because he helps us see. Through him, we learn what our individual life mission is. He shows us who we really are and what we are really doing here in this lifetime.

This is deep but it's not heavy. That's because the *tzaddik* also teaches us the art and science of joy. There is one overarching path to joy: Strengthen *emunah*. When we are joyful, truly joyful, it is a sign that we have genuine faith in God. When we are joyful it shows that we understand that God created everything. Our happiness is evidence that we know that God is sustaining and giving each of us exactly what we need to come closer to Him and to complete our life mission.

Rebbe Nachman's teachings are important to learn because they begin to awaken in us the belief that we can reach our true potential. We can't reach it if we feel depressed or down, or feel that our mission is an unbearable burden. It must be with sweetness and joy.

May you have a day of authentic joy.

You've Got the Power and the Right

R ebbe Nachman teaches us something amazing about anger and unkindness. He tells us that anger and unkindness come about when people have limited knowledge and understanding. When they aren't able to apply what they've learned intellectually. When they aren't able to look in the mirror and see who they are. When this is the state a person is in, the negative imagination takes hold.

All kinds of negative fantasies arise in a person's mind. She might, for example, imagine that another person is less worthy than she. Or he might imagine that another person is trying to take something away from him or trying to harm him. Or she might imagine another person doesn't like her. These are hallucinations! These are the fruits of the negative imagination which can lead to anger and cruelty.

Fortunately, there's a fix. When a person studies the teachings of the *tzaddikim* and begins to get insights into himself, he can start to apply these teachings. When he starts to apply these teachings to every aspect of his life, he starts to bring love and peace into this world. Then anger diminishes. Cruelty and unkindness dissipate.

When you make what you learn real, you have the power to bring peace and love into the world. You have the power to banish your negative fantasies and your anger and cruelty.

May you have a day in which you exercise your power and your right to bring peace and love into the world.

You Are Not Stuck

R eb Noson wrote that freewill is an absolutely astonishing creation. Hashem created us with the ability to choose how we live and whether or not we want to connect with Him.

Somebody once asked Rebbe Nachman about freewill. The Rebbe said it's actually very simple. "If you want, you do. If you don't want, you don't do."

If you think back in time to when perhaps you broke a habit or you made a decision that changed the course of your life, you know that you have great personal power. You changed your life and you changed yourself.

But sometimes we feel that change isn't possible. We feel locked in. *It's not true*. Even a person sitting in jail can make choices about who he is and how he is going to live his life (yes, even behind bars.)

Our life circumstances and our situations are given to us by *Hashem*, not to limit us, but in order to encourage us to see beyond them. When we look at the challenges in our lives and we believe that despite the challenges, or maybe even because of them, we are able to make a choice about how we want to live and who we want to be, we've got real power. We've activated our free will.

May you have a day in which you believe
in your power to make a choice.

Fresh Start

Rebbe Nachman accustomed himself to starting over again – as often as he felt he needed to. Whenever he fell from his present spiritual level, he wouldn't give up. He would simply say: "I will act as if I am just beginning to devote myself to God for the very first time". And then he'd start over again. This happened throughout his life. The Rebbe would slip from his particular elevated level. Then he would pick himself up and start over. He told his followers that sometimes he would do this many, many times each day.

This is a lesson with which you can encourage yourself. You might make a mistake once or twice (or even many times) a day. You might slip. You might look in the wrong direction. You might lose your temper. You might choose to do something you wish you hadn't. If this is the case, you must tell yourself: I'm going to start over. I'm going to make a fresh start. I'm going to try to do better.

After you have made *teshuva* for your errors, there is no point in beating yourself up about the past. Whether that past is a year ago,

a month ago, or five minutes ago, the key is to encourage yourself
to start all over again.

May you have a day of fresh starts.

Banish Money Worries

Rebbe Nachman teaches that one of the causes of depression is an unhealthy desire for money. When a person is caught up in the lust for money, she will also have anxiety and worry about money. All of this anxiety reveals a lack of *emunah*. She doesn't believe that Hashem is giving her what she needs at this moment in time. She doesn't believe that He is the one who supplies everything she has. She thinks that if she works harder or invests smarter or worries more that she'll get more. She forgets that her actions create a vessel into which *Hashem* is the one pouring the *bracha* of sustenance. In truth, He can pour this sustenance into any vessel.

Rebbe Nachman teaches us how to be smart about money. He says that an unhealthy attitude towards money can actually impact a person's health and vitality. If a person has an unhealthy attachment to money, her whole body can become heavy and weak. She'll feel drained. Even her pulse will become weak. This all comes from running after money, says Rebbe Nachman. You can actually risk your life if money becomes your focus!

The Rebbe says there is a way to reverse this degradation of health and happiness. Be aware that if you are highly focused on money, you are far away from *emunah*. But if you understand that you are indeed far away, and yet you still believe in your tremendous potential for spiritual connection, you can begin to repair this breach.

The Rebbe says: *Give a big sigh, take a deep breath.* An honest sigh of profound regret is the technique for curing this downward spiral. You must groan with regret when you realize that you are far away from having true faith. You must moan when you recognize that you don't truly believe that it is Hashem who supplies every iota of your wealth and health. You must sigh when you understand that you are not living up to your faith-potential.

This sigh will strengthen your pulse. It will invigorate you and flood you with high-grade fuel. It will enable you to start over again. You will be able to renew your faith in *hashgacha pratit*, in the belief that Hashem supervises every little thing, including your income.

It's simple, really: An unhealthy obsession with money leads to depression and poor health. Remembering that all sustenance comes from Hashem leads to joy and good health.

> *May you have a day in which you renew your*
> *faith in the Source of your sustenance.*

Unblock and Heal Mind, Body and Soul

E ach person is an entire world, a unique universe filled with potential. Each of us has the power to express Godliness by drawing down holy spiritual energy into our world via our body. When we are able to draw down this spirituality into our eyes, ears, heart, lungs, stomach, feet, etc., we are then able to express and radiate Godliness into our own personal world. We also radiate Godliness into the world at large.

When we don't draw down holy spiritual energy, we are blocked. When we learn how to draw down this holy spirituality, we unblock and heal our mind, body, and soul. Rebbe Nachman teaches how important *halacha* is to attaining this spiritual flow. *Halacha* shares an etymological root with *halicha*, which means walking. When we walk the path prescribed by the Creator, we function optimally.

No one is perfect, which is why Rebbe Nachman tells everyone to adopt the practice of reviewing some *halacha* every day. The *halachot* are the guidelines for the *mitzvot*. When you want to do a *mitzvah* such as making a blessing on food or giving charity and you aren't sure how to do it, you can find the answer in *halacha* texts or by asking someone in the know.

When we do the *mitzvot* according to *halacha*, we make a Divine connection. It's like plugging an appliance into an outlet with the correct voltage and flipping on the switch – voila! You're filled with the light of spirituality which radiates throughout all the worlds.

May you have a day of holy connection.

Philosophy

f you've ridden on the New York City subway during the past few years you might have noticed advertisements for free introductory lessons at a philosophy school. Every time I see these ads, I am reminded of Rebbe Nachman's warning: Avoid philosophy texts and philosophical investigations of all kinds! He explains that the result of philosophizing is an easy road to losing your *emunah*. *Emunah* is the foundation of your life. It is the foundation of your relationship with Hashem. Without it, there is confusion and despair.

It's important that we think and do everything with total simplicity and honesty, says the Rebbe. We should eschew sophistication. One type of sophistication is philosophy. Philosophy, says much of the world, is a noble pursuit.* In reality, the answers to many philosophical questions are beyond the limits of the human intellect. There are many questions that can't be answered at all, or can only be answered with very weak answers, which can be shot down very quickly. Especially questions about God and Creation. The reason

---

*Most philosophy leads to either atheism or idolatry. The Rebbe's advice is gold.

why we can't think our way to the answers is because Hashem is greater than the limits of our human intellect. Hashem is beyond and above all limitations. When we have sincere questions and we hit a wall, *emunah* needs to step in.

What if we have questions that can't be answered satisfactorily and we can't tap into the power of *emunah*? Take a break. Don't push your thoughts in circles. Ask Hashem to help you understand. Listen to some uplifting music. Relax your mind. Either the answer will come eventually from somewhere or the question will cease to bother you.

May you have a day in which you turn to faith
when you reach a philosophical impasse.

Be Happy, Think Clearly

Rebbe Nachman teaches that the main reason why we feel far away from Hashem (and why we don't feel that it's possible to come closer to Him), is because we don't have peace of mind. In order to come close to Hashem we need to be calm and think clearly. Rebbe Nachman says that there is a way to develop peace of mind, even when things are topsy-turvy: Choose to be happy.

When a person is happy, he is able to control and direct his thoughts. He can think about life beyond this worldly existence. He leaves exile and comes to a place of personal freedom. The real exile is in the mind. When a person leaves exile and feels joy, he attains peace of mind.

Happiness is essential in order to have healthy thoughts, to have big-picture thoughts. Happiness is necessary for clear thinking. It is also a choice. Most of us are taught from a very young age that happiness is something that happens to us. Others tell us that if things go right for us, and the things that we want to see happen do happen, then we will be happy. This makes our happiness dependent upon other people and external situations.

Rebbe Nachman says something different. You can make the choice to be happy no matter what is going on. Knowing you can choose happiness gives you freedom and clarity of thought. It helps you face anything that is going on in your life, even the difficulties, with equanimity. When you are able to think about the big-picture stuff including your relationship with Hashem, you gain perspective.

May you have a day of real happiness.

Don't Wait for Inspiration— Express Yourself!

R ebbe Nachman says that the great *tzaddikim* reached their high spiritual levels solely because of *hitbodedut*. They spoke to Hashem in their own words, expressing what was on their minds and in their hearts. The Rebbe says every person should set aside a certain amount of time each day to talk to Hashem.

What happens when you're blocked? There are times when you don't feel able to articulate what is going on inside, or you're feeling impatient and not in the mood. *Hitbodedut* doesn't need to wait for inspiration. If you're feeling blocked ask Hashem for help. You may say something like: *Hashem open my heart to you. Allow me to express what I'm feeling deep down inside. Help me to come closer to You. Help me find the words to talk to you, God.*

Ideally, a person should be talking to Hashem all day long. A person should be talking about whatever is going on in his life. Still, we're busy living our lives, having conversations with other people. We're busy taking care of business. Therefore, we don't really have the presence of mind to do this. This is why Rebbe Nachman says to set aside a specific amount of time each day in which to talk to God. You don't have to worry about the ideal amount of time when you first start. A consistent, few minutes each day is enough to begin to unburden your heart to Hashem. Ask Him to help you come close to Him.

I've seen miracles with people who felt distant from Hashem. They felt unsure of what they believed. They were filled with doubt. Just by speaking to Hashem, whether they were into it or not, spiritual vistas opened up before them. Their lives took on more positive directions.

May you have a day in which you can find the words
to speak what is in your heart to Hashem.

How to Deal with Arguments and Conflict

L ife is hard enough without being involved in conflict and controversy. Rebbe Nachman tells us that the whole world is filled with arguments. Nations quarrel with nations and go to war. Each state and city have many factions, and few seek to compromise. In communities, it's neighbor against neighbor. Within families, husbands argue with wives and children fight with each other.

Why do we fight? What is the reason? If we are pulled into an argument, we might blame the other person's jealousy, entitlement or bad attitude. If we pursue a conflict, we believe that we are nobly fighting for an important principle.

The real reason for all arguments is that nobody thinks about the ultimate purpose of life. Or, if they do think about it, they don't think about it all that much. The Rebbe tells us that a person dies every day, because the day that we already lived isn't coming back. Each day we come a bit closer to leaving this world. We must ask: how can I waste my time on conflict? The Rebbe tells us that anyone who has any sense at all should understand this and win long life for himself. If you waste your time on quarrels, you drain your life away.

Every night before we go to sleep, we forgive everyone. We tell Hashem we don't hold a grudge in our hearts and we don't want anyone punished on our account. How many times do you say these words in the *siddur* and really mean them? Before you go to sleep, it's good to be at peace with everyone, even if that peace is only in your heart for now.

Rebbe Nachman says: *Control yourself and hold your anger.* Live peaceably with everyone even if you didn't start the argument, even if you're on the receiving end. Sometimes someone else has an irrational or unreasonable bone to pick with you. (Sometimes they may be right, we must be open to this, too.) Maybe, they are even jealous. It happens. Don't hate that person in your heart. Forgive them. Understand that this person is just the messenger from Hashem. For some reason you had to go through this quarrel or difficulty. Try your best not to blame the person at all.

It's not easy. Letting go of this kind of painful grudge goes a long way toward making peace, not only in your heart, but also in the world. There is nothing better than peace and seeing good in everyone and getting along with people even if it's not your fault. Do your best to make peace. You will be blessed.

May you have a day in which you turn away from conflict.

Tales of the Tzaddikim

ebbe Nachman says that it is very good to tell stories about the *tzaddikim*. It can help us purify our thoughts. Also, there are certain *tzaddikim* who tell stories in such a way that they bring about dramatic changes in the Universe. It is also good for ordinary people to talk about the lives of the *tzaddikim*, to discuss how they lived their lives.

Rebbe Nachman is so generous with his life. He shares himself with us so openly. He does something that other *tzaddikim* haven't done. Throughout his teachings, he discusses his own process of personal growth. He shares his flaws. He shares his errors. He learned from his mistakes and we can also learn from his mistakes. He tells us that each of us must make our own individual version of this spiritual journey.

Telling stories of the life of Rebbe Nachman and other *tzaddikim* is beneficial, describing both the miracles and the more ordinary facts. Get yourself some books, some collected tales of *tzaddikim* or any of the books about Rebbe Nachman's life.* Make it a practice once or twice a week to sit with your family or friends and read some of these tales.

Many people have the custom of doing this at *seudah shlishit*, the third meal on *Shabbat* afternoon, or after *Shabbat* during the *malaveh malka*. Choose any time that works for you and make it your custom. The stories of the *tzaddikim* will inspire you and bring you to joy. When you are joyful you are able to come closer to Hashem.

May you have a day where you are inspired by the true tzaddikim.

---

* *Sichot HaRan* (*Rebbe Nachman's Wisdom*, BRI); *Chayey Moharan* (*Tzaddik*, BRI); *Through Fire and Water* (a biography of Reb Noson with stories about Rebbe Nachman's life, too, BRI).

Business Matters

R ebbe Nachman teaches that when it comes to business, we should be straightforward and honest. We shouldn't go out of our way to force business deals (or any other kinds of deals.) We should be patient. We should do just the appropriate amount of work necessary to create a structure for the deal to go through.

Most people feel that if they push, and push hard, they will be able to force a deal into place, whether it's a business deal or a personal situation. The truth is that Hashem arranges all types of agreements and connections, including those in the realm of business. He makes all kinds of matches. If we are patient and just do the basics needed to achieve what we need to achieve, then things will happen in their own time. Our job is to create the vessel into which God can pour the blessings, while remembering the outcome isn't up to us at all. It's up to Hashem. That's why we rely on Him with simple *emunah* and *bitachon*.

This is the business advice recommended by Rebbe Nachman. This is what's recommended by all the true *tzaddikim*, scholars, mystics and *kabbalists*. When we think we're the ones in charge, we lose out. We may end up facing tremendous backlash from acting excessively or trying to manipulate, scheme or control. Take a deep breath and trust in Hashem.

May you have a day of successful and easy connections.

Like A Newborn

Our sages say that someone who comes to convert to Judaism is like a newborn baby. The same is true of someone who is born a Jew, but decides to return to her deepest, truest self by returning to Hashem. But when someone wants to enter into the holiness of the Jewish people, the past can be very heavy and cumbersome. It can be a terrible burden.

Rebbe Nachman says anyone who feels like this should strengthen herself and tell herself: *I was born today. I was born today!*

Forget the moments and days from the past. Forget the years. From now on, from this moment on, just live with this thought in mind: *I will cling to Hashem.* I will cleave to the advice and teachings of the holy *tzaddikim.* With these thoughts, you will be able to heal and rectify your past. When you take one step at a time towards good, you will transform those difficult times, even the darkest times, into genuine good.

May you have a day where you remember
that you are like a newborn babe.

93

The Gift of the Yetzer Hara

Reb Noson tells us that when *Moshiach* is revealed, there will still be an evil inclination. That's because a person without a *yetzer hara* is like a dead person, it's as if he doesn't exist. Without his *yetzer hara*, a person has no ability to make choices. He has no free will. Without the *yetzer hara*, the Messiah would be out of work.

Part of *Moshiach's* job is going to be helping us rectify the way we deal with our own negative inclinations. He is going to teach each of us how to come closer to Hashem and how to make choices that truly support the unique nature of our individual soul.

Later in the redemption process, there will come a point in time when the *yetzer hara* will be completely destroyed. There will no longer be a need for people to be corrected and rectified. At that point, all of creation is going to see the incredible beauty of coming close to God. Each person will yearn to connect to God and will seek ways to reveal His Glory. Everyone is going to be filled with cosmic joy and enthusiasm. It will be like graduation and commencement of the next level of existence.

Don't forget that for now, the *yetzer hara* serves a valuable purpose. Without it you wouldn't have free will. You wouldn't be able to choose between right and wrong, good and not good. What a precious gift the *yetzer hara* is.

May you have a day in which you appreciate
your freewill and use it wisely.

It's Always Something – So Why Get Angry?

E very day we potentially face confusion. We're going along. We're in the flow. Maybe we've already faced some obstacles and overcome them. Then, without warning, something comes along and upsets our day. Maybe an hour later something else comes along and upsets our week. We start to feel anger rise – anger at the friend who was late, at the coworker who messed up, or the spouse who failed to follow through on a task.

Sometimes these obstacles are small and feel at least somewhat manageable. Sometimes they are big and feel truly unmanageable. We start to feel like we can't get through the situation we're in. Our thought process starts to break down. Our minds swirl. We become troubled. We have a hard time praying. We feel as if we can't even talk to *Hashem*, though of course, He's the very One who we must turn to in order to find relief.

Rebbe Nachman teaches that the way to get through these upsetting situations is to be very slow to anger. If you are slow to anger it really means that you have *emunah*. If you have *emunah*, then when things come along that might possibly throw you for a loop or drive you up a wall, you'll have a different way of looking at things. You'll immediately remind yourself that everything is from Hashem. You'll remind yourself that this is a test of the *yetzer hara*. It's trying to upset your balance. It's trying to confuse you. It's trying to make you feel that there is no way out. But you will know that there is always a way out.

If we are slow to anger and are committed to being patient, we will endure all the things that come along to annoy and upset us, distract us and drive us crazy. We won't get angry because we'll be able to tap in to the power of Hashem's strength and love. We can literally borrow His Strength. We can borrow His Love, too. Keep this in mind next time something frustrating comes up. (Something always does.)

May you have a day where you are slow to anger.

Hearing is Believing

95

We get vitality from praying. It infuses us with life and faith. But in order to reap the benefits of prayer, generally, we must say the prayers loudly enough so that we can hear them. Even the silent prayers aren't really silent.*

Rebbe Nachman teaches that we should invest some energy into carefully listening to and hearing the words of the prayers we say, especially the personal prayers of *hitbodedut*. We should also hear the words of our prayers from the *siddur*. He recommends we put all our strength into enunciating the prayers clearly, syllable by syllable, word by word, paying attention to the simple meaning of the words. When the prayers enter our ears and we truly hear the words, the prayers then enter our mind and heart. When they do, they rejuvenate us.

---

*During the standing, silent *Amidah* (see a *siddur*) we pray just loudly enough so that we can hear it, but no one else can. Before we begin the first blessing, we also say a brief prayer that asks God to open our lips so our mouths can fully express our prayer.

Next time you are ready to pray think about preparing yourself in advance. Before you pray, say a little prayer asking that you are able to maintain your focus on pronouncing the words correctly. Ask that you are able to say your prayers clearly and loudly enough so that you can hear them. Hearing is believing.

May you have a day where you reap the benefits of your prayers.

96

Knock Down the
Walls of Your Heart

Rebbe Nachman says we should be able to feel another person's troubles in our heart. This is especially true when more than one person is suffering, such as a group or community. Yet, it's perfectly possible to witness that another person is in anguish and still not feel it. Maybe our hearts feel impenetrable. Maybe it's too scary to feel their pain and we'd rather keep our distance.

Today we recognize the need for healthy boundaries. We recognize the need to be able to say no when appropriate. However, it's far better to err on the side of having weak boundaries and feeling another's pain, rather than to close up and not feel for others at all. Rebbe Nachman says that when an entire community is in distress, we must surely feel its agony in our hearts. If we don't, he says, we should strike our head against the wall in order to feel their pain! This means we should strike our head against the walls of our heart. We must bring the realization of another's difficulty from our intellectual minds into our feeling hearts.

He says: Understand this well. There is something about having empathy, having compassion, that transcends the act of giving and helping. We have to do both – we have to give help, but we must also feel. There is something special about really being able to relate to another. That something is what makes us human.

May you have a day in which you think, feel and give.

Your Smile Brings Life

Rebbe Nachman teaches that when you give a person happiness you give a person life. He says that a person can suffer terribly and not be able to express to anyone what's in her heart. There is no one she can connect to. She walks around feeling pained and terribly worried. She's afraid. If you come to such a person and you are smiling, if you have a happy face, you can literally give her life. Rebbe Nachman says this is not an empty gesture. It's a very great thing.

The *Talmud* describes a Persian marketplace. A rabbi was walking through it with Eliyahu HaNavi. He asked the prophet who at the marketplace would merit to reach the World to Come. Eliyahu HaNavi pointed at two men walking by. He told the rabbi: *These two men are jesters and they make people laugh. They will be able to bypass gehinnom and go straight to heaven because they gave joy to others and relieved their hearts.**

*Talmud Ta'anit 22A

It's true that smiling when someone is suffering isn't always appropriate. But, if you can allow someone to unburden themselves to you, or you can tell a joke that makes someone laugh, then you can lift a little bit of their heaviness and suffering. You can infuse them with fresh life.

May you have a day where you are able to shine and share your smile with others.

98

Take A Refreshing Breath (and Don't Get Angry)

We're taught that there are thirteen attributes of mercy of *Hashem*. Rabbi Moshe Cordovero explains that by emulating God and applying the thirteen attributes of mercy to our own lives, we bring healing to our soul and the world. One of *Hashem's* thirteen attributes is *"erekh apayim"*. This attribute, "slow to anger", is an essential personality trait each of us can cultivate.

Erekh apayim, which is literally translated as "long-nosed", can also be translated as "very long breath." In order to control anger a person needs to take a deep long breath. Then with that refreshing breath, he can step back and cool off. He becomes patient and doesn't lose his temper.

Rebbe Nachman says that when a person takes a deep breath in the form of a profound sigh of yearning, this draws down a fresh spirit of life into the person. Whatever he lacks will be rectified. Patience and loving kindness. The ability to forgive. The ability to let go of anger, grudges and resentment. To let go of jealousy and hatred. The deep breath makes a space for these qualities to grow and for other blessings to come down.

The truth is that it's pretty easy to get angry. But there's a deeper, more important truth. If we realize that every experience we have comes from Hashem, we begin to approach *erekh apayim*. If we remember that people who push our buttons are merely agents of Hashem, and we're able to accept what's happening with a measure of equanimity, we're expressing *erekh apayim*.

May you have a day in which you honor your ability to be patient, forgiving and kind.

99

Holy Thought Replacement

There is an incredible teaching of Rebbe Nachman's that will change your life. It really changed mine. *It is the teaching that it is absolutely impossible for a person to have two thoughts at the same time.*

You can test this principle for yourself. Try to think two thoughts at the exact same time. You'll find you cannot. This knowledge gives you a tremendous edge. If you have a negative or destructive thought, just replace it with a positive one. Believe you have the power to change your thoughts by replacing a fearful, anxious, angry, jealous, bitter or depressed thought with any positive thought you choose. Replacing a thought is a more effective way of changing your thoughts than the affirmation method.* Not only does it change *what* you think about, it changes *how* you think.

---

*The positive affirmation method is repeating, out loud and/or in your thoughts, a positive statement such as "I can achieve anything I set my mind to," many times, until it changes your way of thinking about yourself and your life. Although the affirmation method has some benefits, especially if used in conjunction with prayer, it often employs superficial constructs that can end up limiting the depth of your spiritual growth.

There are two things you need to do in order to apply this method:
1. Cultivate awareness of the negative thought cycle in your mind.
2. Replace your energy-draining thoughts with calm, life-affirming ones.

In order to cultivate awareness, you must recognize that you think constantly, even if you aren't aware of it.

Sometimes it's easy to confuse a thought with a feeling or emotion. If you start to experience a negative feeling, it was precipitated by a negative thought. Notice how you feel. If it's negative, pay attention to your thoughts. Slow them down so you can see what the issue is, what you're thinking about. Now, for the second part. Replace your negative thought with a positive thought. Repeat the positive thought over and over again, in your head (or out loud) until it "sticks." You will be able to literally turn your thoughts in another direction with this technique.

You don't have to be a deep or original thinker to use thought replacement. In fact, sometimes the best thoughts aren't our own. We are blessed with a tremendous line-up of uplifting, comforting and inspiring thoughts in Judaism. You can take a verse or two from Psalms, a line or two from Rebbe Nachman's teachings in *Likutey Moharan* or a few bits of the prayers from the *siddur* or Reb Noson's collection of prayers.*

You can turn to these texts or others when you are having negative thoughts, or better yet, prepare in advance. Find some texts (a phrase or sentence or two) that you truly believe and trust, and have them ready. Compile a list of go-to replacement thoughts. The next time your mind is going in a direction that doesn't feel positive, read one of those lines to yourself. It will drive the other

---

* *The Fiftieth Gate (Likutey Tefillot)* is a sensitive and beautiful English translation of Reb Noson's prayers, published by the Breslov Research Institute.

thoughts out of your head. You may have to do this several times until you get the hang of it, but it's truly worth it.

Here's an example: A lot of people can't go to sleep at night because their thoughts race. Or they wake up in the middle of the night and worry. This isn't so unusual. If this has happened to you, perhaps you instinctively tried to change your thoughts. This was smart. So you got out of bed, read a novel or watched a movie to take your mind off your worries. The truth is, this probably worked! But it's a short-term solution. If you want something that not only is effective immediately, but also improves your thoughts over time, borrow some holy sentences from King David or Rebbe Nachman or other true *tzaddikim*.

Eventually, you'll have memorized some positive thoughts and this will lead you to create new positive thoughts that originate from your personal *nekuda tova*.

May you have a day filled with positive thoughts.

100

Break Your
Heart of Stone

Once upon a time a king sent his son to study the wisdoms of the world. The prince spent many years becoming well versed in all the arts and sciences. Finally he returned home. When the king saw him, he said, "My beloved son, I want you to do me a particular favor. You see that mountain? There's a big stone at the bottom. I'd like you to bring it up to the top." With that, the king returned to his chambers.

The prince was truly grateful to his father and wanted to fulfill his wishes. But the stone was as big as a millstone. It was so heavy that he couldn't even budge it. He sat down at the bottom of the mountain and cried. Eventually, the king returned and said, "My beloved son, do you really think that I wanted you to do the impossible? To carry this stone to the top of the palace just as it is? Even with all your wisdom how could you do such a thing? Take a hammer and smash the stone into tiny pieces. Carry it piece by piece to the top of the mountain."

Hashem tells us to lift our heart up to the heavens. But life is hard and we are overwhelmed with doubts and confusion. All our wisdom and the wisdom of the world cannot help. Our heart is a heart of stone. It's impossible to raise it up except by taking a hammer and breaking it into little tiny pieces. Rebbe Nachman teaches us that the hammer is speech, especially prayer. When we talk to *Hashem* in our own words and express what is on our mind and in our heart, this is how we break the heart of stone inside us. This is how we lift our hearts up and connect with God. This is prayer.

May you have a day in which you are able to express your most heartfelt thoughts and feelings in prayer.

101

Finding What You've Lost

S ome people live their lives like leaves in the wind. Whichever way the wind blows, they float and flutter. Other people live their lives like rocks stuck in the mud. No matter what is happening around them, they remain immobile and rigid.

Yet we know that people have free will. They are able to choose a goal. They are able to make an impact on the world around them. They are able to change themselves. But in order to fully exercise the highest form of free will, each of us must understand what our life is about and where we're headed.

The sages explain that before we are born, when our souls are still up above, we are taught everything we need to know about our lives. We are taught what we need to accomplish in this lifetime. But the moment we are born and we take our first breath, we forget everything. If we don't try and remember our mission, we lose so much of our lives. If we don't try and find what we've lost, we can end up like a leaf or a rock.

Rebbe Nachman tells us that by connecting with his wisdom we can uncover what we have lost. His teachings are designed to help us discover our personal life mission. He gives us the knowledge that will help us accomplish what we need to accomplish in this lifetime. The main tools we use in order to apply his teachings are learning and prayer. Rebbe Nachman gives us hundreds of lessons to learn. Reb Noson, the primary disciple of Rebbe Nachman, who is known for spreading his teachings, also gives us hundreds of prayers to say (prayerful-meditations that ask for spiritual assistance in applying Rebbe Nachman's lessons.) By learning and praying we can begin to peel back the confusion of this world. We can reveal what we've forgotten. We can find the holy inspiration that we've lost.

Then, we won't flutter in the wind. We won't hunker down and turn into stone. We will truly be able to decide which way to go.

May you have a day in which you remember who you truly are.

Talk to A Gun

Sometimes you come before God and want to talk to Him, but you can't find the words. You don't know what to say. You feel blocked. Rebbe Nachman says that even if a person can't speak at all, he can still say something. For example, you could say, *Ribono shel Olam*, (Master of the Universe), over and over again. Repeat this or something simple until you get unstuck. The Rebbe says you might even spend many days saying one thing – and that's okay. If you are persistent and repeat a holy idea many, many times, Hashem will have mercy on you and help you express what's on your mind and in your heart.

Why is it so easy to chat with friends, or pick up the phone and call someone, or schmooze with a neighbor? Why is that so easy? Why is it so hard to express our deepest inner truths, whether to other people or *Hashem*? It's because true speech is very potent. It's so effective that really, a person should spend the entire day in *hitbodedut*, says Rebbe Nachman. But today, people can't do this. Therefore, we have to talk to Hashem as much as we are able.

The key is consistency. Even if it's just a few minutes a day, if you are committed to the practice, two minutes will turn into three, and three into four. Before you know it, you will be making significant strides in the amount of time you spend talking to God. It's worthwhile doing so. Rebbe Nachman says that if a person actually knows how, he can talk to a gun so it won't shoot.

> *May you have a day in which you believe enough in the power of your speech that you make time to talk to God.*

Should You Go Fast or Slow?

Rebbe Nachman teaches that when a person who has been on the path of righteousness and closeness to God his whole life goes from *mitzvah* to *mitzvah*, he should do so at a measured pace. Then he will be able to perceive and experience the holiness that is found in each *mitzvah*.

But what about people who are new to the path? For these people, Rebbe Nachman says, (and he uses strong language): *It's forbidden to relax or linger when going from mitzvah to mitzvah.* Instead, a person like this must run, skip and jump into holiness. They must do it with great speed and zeal. A person like this is rewarded for their *zerizut.* Whereas a person with a lot of *mitzvot* in the bank, so to speak, loses out, a person new to the path must hurry to catch up.

So where are you holding? Should you go slowly and immerse yourself? Or should you run and leap with alacrity? In order to really know what's best for you, you have to be able to evaluate yourself. You'll need to analyze this in the context of Jewish wisdom. For this, you'll need to grab some books, get a teacher or two, and learn. The fact that you are willing to assess yourself is in and of itself, great merit.

May you have a day in which you act zealously when necessary or go slowly when necessary.

104

Serving Hashem with your Negative Side

ebbe Nachman tells us that the essence of *teshuva*, totally returning to Hashem, His Torah, and one's true self, is when a person is able to pass through the same minefields of temptation into which he previously stumbled, and this time not fall in thought or deed. This is complete *teshuva*.

So why do we have to navigate these minefields of temptation in the first place? Rebbe Nachman tells us something incredible. He says it's actually a good thing when a person still has an evil inclination, the lust to do something negative. Why is this a good thing? Because a person can serve Hashem through his *yetzer hara*.

A person who prevails against the fiery power of his evil inclination, who doesn't give in and who forcibly drags his mind away from tempting thoughts,* is living his faith. A person who turns all of his attention, even momentarily, towards the light and away from

---

*These thoughts include anger, bitterness, hate, revenge, jealousy, immorality, and other negative urges.

darkness, is serving Hashem with his *yetzer hara* by transcending his *yetzer hara*.

The slightest movement away from negative thoughts is a great victory for holiness.

> *May you have a day in which you believe you can*
> *change your thoughts and inclinations.*

105

Live in the Present

There was a rabbi who used to empty his pockets before going to bed each night, ensuring he was penniless.* All day long he would distribute any money he received to the poor and needy. Each morning, he would wake up and rely totally on *Hashem* to provide his daily sustenance. He did this the way the Jews in the desert relied on *Hashem* to provide the *manna* each day.

Rebbe Nachman says that just as we should live in the present and rely on Hashem to provide our sustenance day to day, we should also focus on our spirituality in the present moment as well. Why?

If we think about what our spiritual tasks will be tomorrow, next week or next month, we will feel overwhelmed. But if we think about only what we have to do today, our spiritual service becomes manageable. We can begin by thinking: Now I have to wake up and thank Hashem. I have to pray. I need to do that now. (If we're advanced, we can also think: Later today I will focus on making a blessing, giving charity, learning Torah—what I need to do then.)

---

*This was a practice of several *tzaddikim*.

Rebbe Nachman says this is the best way to serve *Hashem*. Just live in the moment. Part of this is also learning how not to push off what really does need to be done today. Don't say: Tomorrow I am going to commit to a spiritual path, tomorrow I'm going to do *mitzvot*. No – do it now! Just do it and you'll accomplish.

May you have a day in which you accomplish what's important in the present moment, with joy.

Magic

A couple of decades ago a children's book was published that had such an effect on the publishing world, dozens and dozens of spin-offs, copycat books and movies were spawned. Even today, people who have no interest in children's literature have heard of "Harry Potter." The book is about a little boy who uses sorcery and witchcraft to control his world and vanquish his enemies. Why is this book so popular even now?

Reb Noson tells us that many people are superstitious. They believe in (or wish they could believe in) magic, sorcery, omens, signs, astrology, and fortune-telling. They want to find a way to control their world and vanquish their enemies. They're faced with all kinds of questions and problems. They don't know which course of action to take. They don't know what to choose. They are confused and plagued with doubt.

Doubt is actually an intense form of suffering.

Though it's true some people are ruled by their feelings, we all rely at least part of the time on our intellect. The problem is that our intellect is limited. For example, we can't see the future. We can make certain logical inferences that can lead to somewhat reliable predictions, but much of life is uncertain. We feel if only we could work things out with knowledge and logic, we'd be safe. If we rely on our intellect there is always an element of doubt, so this is why some people turn to things like astrology, magic and gurus. Still, the inability to make perfect choices and control most things in life defines a large part of the human condition. Wishful thinking and sorcery won't help.

In the world beyond this one, there is unity. There is Oneness. When there is Oneness there is no need to make choices because Oneness is indivisible. There are no options but one. That Oneness is *Hashem*. Reb Noson explains during our lifetime, we should work on perceiving and connecting to that Oneness. Then much of our confusion and doubt fades away.

When you're not sure what to do, keep the ultimate goal in mind – and remember *Hashem's* Oneness. Turn to the advice of the *tzaddikim* who are able to guide you through the *Torah*. When you make a decision based on this kind of advice, if it goes well for you, and everything looks good, then wonderful. If the outcome doesn't look good, if the blessings are hidden, at least you'll know you did the right thing.

May you have a day where your choices are clear.

More Free Will

Rebbe Nachman says that everything you see in this world, everything in creation, from a snail to a toll both, from the Kalahari Desert to a rain cloud, was created for the sake of free will. The entire reason for creation is to enable us to make choices.

What is free will? The Rebbe said it's very simple. "If you want, you do. If you don't want, you don't do". Reb Noson explains that a lot of people are confused because they are used to the idea that they're in chains. Their habits and desires chain them up. They don't feel free to choose their actions. They feel they can't control the way they live.

The truth is, no matter what our circumstances are, we have the power to choose. Reb Noson also explains that we have a special power. We can choose any idea or piece of advice that we hear, we can grab hold of it, and we can make it our own. If it's good, we can apply it to our lives – and benefit. Go ahead, take one little idea, and change your life with it! This is an incredible amount of power.

Exercising our free will is the mechanism by which we live. Think about it: You are constantly making choices. You make simple choices such as what to eat for dinner or what to wear that day. You make more complex choices that will have ramifications on your material future, such as whether or not to choose a particular career or marriage partner. Then you make other, vital choices, essential to both your material and spiritual wellbeing: Should I pray? Should I give charity? Should I come closer to God?

You are given choices. But then, it's up to you. Rebbe Nachman says: *Put your energy into choosing good.*

May you have a day in which you are aware of your options.

108

Creating Peace and Forgiveness

I f there is a lack of peace between people, they can't come close to *Hashem*. Rebbe Nachman explains that when peace prevails, when we get along with others, we can sit down together and talk. When we have peace, we can open our hearts and encourage and inspire each other. We can talk about our lives and the ultimate purpose of life, which is having a relationship with our Creator.

When there is strife, when there is enmity or jealousy, people are guarded and they don't open their hearts to one another. They can't speak the truth. They can't make themselves vulnerable. They try to one up the other person or they hide. In that case, truth flees and it becomes impossible to have a genuine relationship with others and Hashem. During the days between *Rosh Hashanah* and *Yom Kippur*, we ask each other for forgiveness for anything we might have done to harm or hurt another person. But we don't have to limit this to ten days a year. We can ask for forgiveness and make peace anytime.

Only you know the negative feelings that exist in your heart. Only you can purge those feelings. You can even ask for God's help. Ask him to help you make the pain go away so that you view others with acceptance. Remember: you are a conduit for peace and can help bring the world closer to Hashem.

May you have a day of peace.

109

The Treasure Inside You

Once upon a time there was a man who lived in a little brick house in the countryside. He was very poor. One night he had a dream that there was a treasure under a particular bridge in Vienna. He didn't think much about it. Then he had the dream again the next night. He said to himself, well it's probably just a coincidence. When he had the same dream the third night, he believed there was a message in it.

He packed up his meager belongings, locked up his little brick house, put some food and a spade in his knapsack and walked all the way to Vienna, only stopping to pray, eat and sleep. When he arrived in the big city, he came to the bridge he had seen in his dreams. He pulled out his spade and began to dig. Just then a police officer who had been guarding the bridge clapped him on the shoulder.

"Hey, you, what are you doing digging under my bridge?" said the guard.

The man told him about his dream and the treasure that might be buried there. He said he would split the treasure with him. The police officer laughed and said, "You Jews always dream."

He said that he himself had a dream the other night. He dreamed of a little brick house with a treasure buried deep in the yard. But because he wasn't a foolish Jew but an intelligent police officer, he didn't run off and chase after his dream.

The Jew was astonished. The police officer had described his very own house! He thanked the officer and rushed home. He dug up his yard and sure enough, found the treasure.

"Isn't that amazing?", he thought. "The treasure was right here near me all along. However, in order to find it I had to travel all the way to Vienna."

Rebbe Nachman explains that each person has a hidden treasure, right under his nose. In order to find it, he has to travel to the *tzaddik*. The *tzaddik* will help him find his treasure.

You have a divine treasure inside. You are unique. You are one of a kind. You are integral to the story of the world and nobody can replace you. In order to understand who you are, and in order that you make the most of the treasure within, you must seek someone to guide you. The teachings of the tzaddikim, and especially Rebbe Nachman of Breslov, can help you find the treasure inside.

May you have a day in which you discover
the treasure closest to home.

110

True Freedom

D epression is exile and joy is freedom. When a person is unhappy and depressed her mind goes into exile. It becomes very difficult for her to concentrate on anything important, especially her relationship with *Hashem*. Rebbe Nachman says that the main reason why people don't come closer to *Hashem* is that they are unable to think clearly about their main purpose in life.

If you stop and think a moment, you'll realize that when you are unhappy, it is almost impossible to think clearly. When you are happy your mind is calm. Happiness brings *yishuv hada'at*, settled thoughts and a peaceful mind. Then, you are able to understand things clearly. Peace of mind is expansive. It can create a safe, nurturing space for you to reflect on your life and think about your goals.

The Rebbe tells us we should do our utmost to fill our minds with joy. This way we become freed from the exile of depression. The Rebbe encourages us to believe that *simcha* is a choice. It's something that we can grab hold of. No matter what is going on around us, we can do our best to reject depression and exile and instead choose joy and freedom. Pursue joy and elevate yourself. Rebbe Nachman suggests you sing and dance. Do things to lift your spirits, the things that bring you pure and holy happiness. The way to freedom is joy.

May you have a day of true freedom.

The Gift of Forgetting

Think about some good memories you have. Recall a time when you did something you were proud of. If these were the only memories you had, then forgetting would be a tragedy. But if you recall every time that you said or did something you wish you hadn't, you'd be better off forgetting.

If we recalled everything we regretted, everything we're ashamed of, it would be impossible for us to lift our heads up. The pain could cause a soul-dislocation. That's why some things are best forgotten.

This doesn't mean that when we are feeling stronger, we can't take out those memories one by one and review them. We can speak about them with Hashem and learn from them. We can express remorse and commit to doing better in the future.

However, if your painful, shameful memories are dragging you down; if you feel overwhelmed by the weight of the past, it's okay to set it all aside for the moment. Rebbe Nachman teaches that it is most important to be joyful. Forgetting is an aid to joy. It confers great psychospiritual benefits. It enables you to not only believe in Hashem but also to believe in yourself.

May you have a day of joy and inner strength.

What A Fool Believes

I t says in Proverbs that a fool believes in everything. Rebbe Nachman says it can actually be good to be that kind of fool. Why? If you believe in things even if they are false and foolish, you are developing your faculty of faith and belief. Eventually, because you've exercised your faith-muscles, you'll come around to believing the truth: That *Hashem* created the world and gave us His *Torah*.

If you are a faith-filled fool, you're far better off than a sophisticated skeptic. A sophisticated skeptic goes around ridiculing anything which appears to him to be false and foolish. He is often accurate, because so many things in this world are indeed false and foolish. However, by doing this he develops his faculty of skepticism and ridicule. He gets very good at tearing things down. Eventually, he will deny even the Truth.

The Rebbe reminds us that it is better to be a bit foolish and believe in *Hashem* than to be someone who has no *emunah*.

There's another important lesson intertwined with the one about being a fool. It's that faith isn't something that just occurs. We tend to think that some people just naturally are born with *emunah*. But this is far from the truth. Faith is a habit. Events occur in your life and you see Providence where other people see meaningless coincidences and synchronicities. It's okay to tell yourself (often) that everything that happens to you is from *Hashem*. It's okay to say to yourself: "He arranged that parking spot just for me." Or: "*Hashem* wanted me to run into that person today and hear what she had to say." It's more than okay – it's good. It's good to know that even if you can't understand the way *Hashem* runs the world, you still believe He's running it.

May you have a day in which you see Hashem in everything.

The "Oy" Breath
(Fresh Air)

Rebbe Nachman explains that breathing is not only essential to physical life, it is essential to spiritual life as well. When we breathe in, we need to breathe in both physically and spiritually pure air. When we breathe out, we need to breathe out physically and spiritually impure air.

We all hold onto things that clog us up. With proper breathing you can rid yourself of your emotional sludge, such as pain or bitterness that comes from the things you wish had gone differently for you in your past. The way to do this is to sigh. Take a deep breath in, then sigh out the negative air, through your mouth. It helps to make the sound "oy" as you deeply sigh.

When you breathe in the next breath after that sigh, you're breathing in fresh, pure air. Rebbe Nachman teaches that with that next, new breath, it's as if you're born again. You'll get a new vitality from this act of breathing in and sighing out, breathing in and sighing out. Both soul and body become renewed and refreshed.

Sigh out your negative emotions. Sigh out your feelings of regret for the things you've done that have taken you away from your true spiritual potential. Say "oy" for the things that have led you away from the Creator. Then, breathe in the fresh new air of hope and forgiveness. It's the pure air of starting over. This is something that you can do literally any time of the day. No one has to see you doing it. You can sit in a room full of people and let out a small sigh. Keep in mind that you are expelling negativity, and keep in mind that your next breath in will be one of goodness and joy.

May you have a day of fresh air.

14

You

R ebbe Nachman says that your biggest obstacles are in your mind. You must believe in yourself and push through the undermining thoughts you have about yourself. Sometimes those thoughts are obvious, and sometimes they are deeply hidden. Rout them out and banish them!

Do you understand how important you are and how important your life is? Do you realize your true potential? Each person can achieve her own kind of spiritual greatness, but most of us (perhaps you?) simply don't believe we're capable.

Wake up every day and think about the purpose of your life. This doesn't have to be heavy and weighty and feel like a burden. This can be joyful and light and increase your enthusiasm. The main thing is to recognize who you are and where you are headed. In order to have this awareness, you must believe in your spiritual importance. Believe in the fact that Hashem made only one you. He gave you a unique soul and your soul is accomplishing something in this world that no one else can possibly accomplish.

May you have a day in which you believe in your true potential.

The Company You Keep

We are able to influence others far more than we realize. We also need to be aware that other people can influence us. Sometimes this is apparent, such as when we spend time with an inspiring teacher or mentor and are consciously receptive to their influence. And sometimes this influence is more subtle, such as when we spend time working with a colleague who begins to affect how we think. Sometimes this influence is positive. Sometimes it isn't.

Rebbe Nachman tells us that a person can do more to deter another from connecting to the Creator than the *yetzer hara* itself. For example, mockery and sarcasm about spirituality or *Torah,* no matter how funny or seemingly harmless, can lead both the speaker and the listener to weaken their spiritual connection. The Rebbe tells us to be vigilant about engaging in or listening to this kind of talk.

There are also more subtle ways another person could influence another to disengage from faith and holiness. We all respond to peer pressure to varying degrees. We all want to be liked. We all want to be appreciated. Most people care about what others think of them. This can put you in a vulnerable position. It can be difficult to stand strong if you believe that other people are trying to put you down for what you believe. Remember, if you truly want something, you'll do it. Do you want to be lifted up or dragged down? It is up to you to choose not only who you want to be, but who you want to be with.

May you have a day spent in the company of good and holy friends.

Your Unique Day

ebbe Nachman teaches that each day has its own unique thoughts, words and actions. Each of these is not only unique to that particular day, but each of them is unique to every person. The Rebbe explains that a person should think about all the different situations he finds himself in each day.

When you think about it, no matter how repetitious or uneventful your schedule might be, no matter how similar one day seems to the next, there are important differences. Your thoughts, the words you say and the things you do are different each day. They may be vastly different or they may differ in fine points. Still, there are differences upon differences.

What is going on behind the scenes in the different situations we find ourselves in each day? The Rebbe explains that *Hashem* is sending us hints. He is wrapping hints up into every aspect of every day. The hints are there to help us grow and draw closer to the Creator. How can we access these hints? Take a few minutes at the end of the day when you have the ability to focus, and reflect on everything that has happened.

You can also seize the opportunity to access these hints the moment you experience them. For example, you may suddenly get an appealing new idea. Or something unusual may occur, a "chance" meeting for example. Right then and there stop, take a deep breath and ask yourself: *Here is something different sent to me from God. How can this unique thought or unusual event bring me closer to Him or inspire me to grow?*

This is a way of becoming more aware that *Hashem* supervises everything. It's a way of training yourself to see that you are offered the chance to seek and find Him in every moment. With practice, you will allow this to be part of your conscious awareness.

Look! There is something for you to discover in each moment, even in the repetitious moments, the ones that seem like drudgery. There is something for you in the whirlwind moments, too. Look at the heart of each moment. It doesn't matter who you are or what your situation in life is. It doesn't matter how uneventful your life seems and it doesn't matter if your life is a crazy roller coaster. Hashem is designing your whole day just for you.

May you have a day where you seek and find
Hashem's guidance in the moments.

Toxic Shame vs. Healthy Shame

There are two kinds of shame. The first is toxic shame. This is the shame where we don't really believe or understand that we have a holy *neshama*. We don't feel that we have a connection to Hashem. We don't understand that our lives are vitally and uniquely important to the story of the universe. *We need to heal this shame!*

The way to begin to heal is to look for the *nikudot tovot*, the good points in ourselves (and others.) This concept is discussed at length in Rebbe Nachman's lesson, *Azamra*.

When we look for the good points inside, we come to recognize that our lives are intricately and intimately bound up in our relationship with *Hashem*. We begin to understand that we can make important potential accomplishments in this world, material and spiritual accomplishments.

The other kind of shame is *busha*. You can remember the word because it sounds like "bashful." *Busha* is a holy, healthy type of shame. It's a shame that is the product of humility. The Rebbe himself spoke about his own level of *busha*. He said that when he was alone with God and he would speak to Him, his *busha* was so great that he would actually blush. His face would burn with holy shame. The Rebbe would express himself with tremendous timidity and embarrassment, feeling completely humbled, and even humiliated as he faced the Holy One. This is an especially revealing kind of humility. This humility comes from the willingness to be vulnerable and to trust and love *Hashem*.

Reb Noson said that *busha* shone on the Rebbe's face and nothing like it had ever been seen before. This holy shame is actually very healing. It comes from a place of great honesty. It's the place where our soul can speak her truth. We begin to understand the depth of our relationship with *Hashem* – the dependence and the awe, the trust and the love, once we start to experience this holy shame.

May you have a day where you trust yourself
and Hashem enough to be vulnerable.

Growing Emunah Consciousness

Rebbe Nachman speaks about the importance of *emunah*. He shows us so many pathways to achieving *emunah*. We don't always realize this, but *emunah* is essential to our emotional and mental wellbeing. If a person doesn't have faith in God and doesn't believe that God loves him and wants a relationship with him, he's missing out on the primary source of love and strength. If a person doesn't believe that *Hashem* is directing everything – every moment and each event in his life – and that ultimately, whatever happens is for his personal benefit, she may be prone to despair when things go awry. Or she'll feel like a victim when people disappoint her. Or worse, she may give up.

When a person who has *emunah* hits a rough patch in life, she reminds herself that *Hashem* has surely engineered this particular difficult trial only for her ultimate benefit. He is not doing it to hurt her, God forbid. *Hashem* is giving her obstacles and challenges to help her grow. He is also teaching her to turn to Him for help. And when she does, she will also find new points of strength inside herself which she can then use her entire life.

How does true *emunah* get expressed? The most fundamental and functional way in which you can express *emunah* is to turn to *Hashem* by talking to Him, in good times and rough times. To ask Him for His help, for His advice, for His solace. If you have true *emunah* you will genuinely believe that no matter what you are going through, it is for the ultimate good. You will genuinely believe that *Hashem* is giving you this particular difficulty because He loves you. You will even be able to uncover some hidden joy in the shadows of your problems.

You cannot get to that level of *emunah* right away. It might even seem impossible to you that you may ever get there. You might even get annoyed or angry with the idea that you should trust that your hard times, your painful times, could be for the good. You might feel that someone who suggests this doesn't understand or has never been through heartache.

You might think that *emunah* is something a person has or doesn't have. But, *emunah* isn't something you're born with, it's not in your chromosomes. It's not a passive trait like shyness or red hair. *Emunah* is a potential, like musical or athletic ability. You have to learn the notes and chords of *emunah*. You have to exercise your *emunah* muscles. You have to cultivate, nourish and nurture your *emunah*, otherwise it lies dormant. And that's a waste.

Read stories about people with *emunah*. Spend time with people who have strong *emunah*. Think about the ways in which you think about faith, God, and life, and you will grow your *emunah*.

May you have a day of growing emunah consciousness.

The (Real) Secret

wo important ideas:
1. Our desire is essential to getting what we want.
2. Our thoughts create our reality.

These two concepts go hand-in-hand.

Several years ago, many secular books were published which illustrated the concept that what you think about and what you focus on is what you're going to attract. This became known as the "law of attraction." There is some truth to this idea. But something's missing from the equation. What's missing is the idea that we should strive to desire something that is truly worthy of us. We should desire something that is truly worthy of and befitting beings with a spark of the Divine, beings with a soul.

Here's the *real* secret: When we desire something and focus our thoughts on it, if it's not worthy of us, we won't be satisfied with it when we get it. This is why, for example, after most athletes or celebrities win a game or receive an award, they crash. They'll start to work on the next big thing as soon as possible. They can't enjoy the win too much past the initial moment. It's the creating and doing that's satisfying to them.

However, when our desire has a loftier purpose and when what we desire is befitting our beautiful, holy soul, when we do achieve what we desire, our soul itself receives satisfaction.* Rebbe Nachman teaches us not only how to harness the power of our will and our thoughts, but how to evaluate the content of what we desire and what we focus on. When both work in tandem, a meaningful life is born. Your life.

May you have a day in which you fulfill your most meaningful desires.

---

*Even seemingly mundane or material achievements can also be informed by positive spiritual purpose.

Hidden Remedies

There are times when the Holy One is concealed from us. We don't feel particularly connected to Him. We may yearn for the time when we used to feel connected and close, but at the moment we don't feel that way. During these times we must know we should seek *Hashem* out, whether or not we pray, whether or not we learn *Torah*, whether or not we do *mitzvot*. These will help us to find Him.

Then there are times when there is a concealment within a concealment and *Hashem* is doubly hidden from us. During these times, we don't even realize what is missing. We don't yearn for Him. We don't think about Him. We just live our lives.

Rebbe Nachman teaches us that during a concealment within a concealment, if we honestly do seek *Hashem* out, even if we are not sure what we believe, even if we feel a disconnect or doubt, we will eventually find Him. To seek Him, talk to him in your own words. Say: I don't know what I believe. I have tremendous doubts but I am here, and I'm honestly trying to get to the truth. I am honestly trying to find You.

During these times when we speak to our Creator in truth about what is on our minds and in our hearts, we make that first step in getting closer.

May you have a day in which you know
Hashem is always with you.

Acknowledgments

I t's impossible to adequately thank everyone involved in the creation of this book but I enjoy attempting the impossible, so I'll try:

Without Gavriel (Glenn) and Chana (Candace) Sneider, this and other Breslov projects for women simply wouldn't exist. Their significant material support and deeply warm friendship gave me the material ability, headspace, and heart to write this book. Reb Gavriel's kindness and generosity are boundless. My lovely chavrusa Chana has nurtured this book along in every possible way. The concept for this book was her idea, she asked me to write it, and then, without much ado, proceeded to transcribe hundreds of my talks so I could rewrite them into the format you find on these pages. (The group of transcriptions was the most surprising birthday present I ever received!) She gave sage editing, marketing, and other advice, and constantly encouraged me via email, text, and phone calls. In addition, she hosted me at her beautiful historic home in Newtown, Pa., creating an ergonomic writer's studio overlooking her garden, and supplied me with whatever a writer could possibly need and more: coffee, great conversations, walks through historic Newtown, and a charming view from my writing desk. Chana also took us on an incredible winter-time journey to Uman; the cold was bitter but our hearts were warmed by the fire of Breslov. She invested in the BreslovWoman.org dream and turned it into Breslov Woman, a viable organization for women, spending countless hours filling in forms and other bureaucratic *menios*. As President of Breslov Woman, she's responsible for helping women on their personal journeys to joy and connection, and God willing, she'll be blessed with success.

This book is as much hers as mine —we are partners in recognizing the potential in taking Rebbe Nachman's life-changing insights and offering them up in digestible and practical briefs which are truly able to transform a life. I am filled with gratitude.

Many thanks to Rachelle Ellis and Susan Raskind who gave generously of their time as board members of the nascent Breslov Woman organization. May you both receive many blessings and continue to share the teachings of Rebbe Nachman.

Thanks to Lauren Zahavi whose idea it was for me to do the daily WhatsApp mini-podcasts, upon which this book is based. Thanks to Shulamit Michal (Susan) Strassburger for never saying no to volunteering. Thank you to Dovid and Rosalie Mark for their help with the BreslovWoman.org website and for Rosalie's incredible organizational help with the BRI Uman tour for women (I don't know how I did it without her.) May we be blessed to travel together to Uman again.

Thanks to the many friends (old and new), sponsors, students, and coaching clients, who've inspired me with their friendship, support, and stimulating discussions, whether on the road to Uman, in Eretz Yisrael, or in America. It would take pages to mention everyone, but I'll start with a few: Chezi and Yehudis Gerin; Eliora Yocheved Goodrich; Dorry Siegler Baum; R' Avraham and Rachelle Newman; Mojgan Shokrian; Shira Chana Bienstock; Janice Bienstock; Bina bat Farahnaz; Shayna Franks; Rich and Bea Greenberg; Stacey Gains; Susan (Sara) Kramer; Devorah Kaufman; Libi Astaire; Leah Sarah Chusid; Doris Borg; Jody Teicher; Gitty Stolik; Georganne Garfinkel; Esther Rabizadeh; Michal Miller; Benita Leitner; Chavi Rosenfeld;– if your name isn't here and it should be, please accept my thanks.

Rebbe Nachman teaches that a teacher is inspired to work on themselves through the act of teaching others. This has certainly held true for me. Thanks to everyone who has hosted or sponsored my classes: Reb Gil Bashe, Chairman of the Breslov Research Institute, who has consistently and generously supported women's Breslov programming in New York, New Jersey and Uman, Ukraine. The Breslov Research Institute and Yossi Katz, for hosting my classes around town, at Shabbatons, via tours of Jewish Ukraine, and more. Joel Kleinman of the BOMA shul for sponsoring and hosting Breslov shiurim for women. Rabbi Naftali Citron of the Carlebach Shul, for inviting me to speak for the past five years at the annual Kabbalah Day at the JCC Manhattan. Susie Kessler and everyone at the JCC Manhattan for supporting the Breslov women's contemplative writing workshops, the Azamra program, etc. Devorah Wildey for sponsoring online classes; Sharon Glaser and Ginny Kafka of Congregation Ahavas Yisrael for hosting the Holy Self-Esteem brunch; Debbie Eisikowitz and the Five Towns Women's Lecture Series, along with the Young Israel of Lawrence-Cedarhurst for hosting my leadership class; Rabbi Moshe and Mrs. Scheindy Fischman for their support of the daily WhatsApp lessons; JMAC and Amanda Jones for hosting the Holy Self-Esteem Workshop brunch. Also thanks to the many women who've hosted Breslov classes and workshops for women in their homes: Miriam Pineles, Rivka Sara Borukhov, Maya Batash, Tzvia Chanie Silbiger, Yehudit Meira Chervony, and many others. There are more hosts and sponsors than I can list here, please know you are appreciated.

Many thanks to my powerhouse friend and student Hillary Barr Markowitz for hosting the Freedom from Fear Workshop in her home, the Passover Inspiration class with the Fifth Avenue Synagogue, and for her enthusiasm, expertise in natural healthcare, and boundless compassion and generosity. May she and her family be blessed with good health, long life, happiness, peace and closeness to Hashem, and may she continue to find inspiration and joy in the teachings of Rebbe Nachman and all our true tzaddikim.

Many thanks to my lovely friend and student Esther Ella Gurevich, for sponsoring the upcoming Breslov classes for women in NYC, IyH, and also for her warm friendship and generosity. She is a rare soul who stands firm for what she believes and does so with grace. May she and her family be blessed with good health, long life, happiness, peace and closeness to Hashem, and may she continue to tap into the merit of sharing the life-changing joy of Rebbe Nachman's teachings. Kol hakavod!

Many thanks to my strong friend and student Dr. Eleonora Goudis for her sponsorship of this book, and for initiating the upcoming Breslov classes for women in NYC, IyH, as well as for her kindness and generosity. Eleonora is a brave and beautiful soul who inspires me all the time. May she and her family be blessed with good health, long life, happiness, peace and closeness to Hashem, and may she continue to tap into the merit of sharing the life-changing joy of Rebbe Nachman's teachings. Kol hakavod!

Many thanks to my sister-friend Simcha Yael (Stephanie) Roth, who is an inspiration, for many reasons, not least of which is her decades-long dedication to the teachings of Rebbe Nachman and for living up to her name with joy. Her proofreading, insightful questions and suggestions made this book more professional and accessible. She also makes me laugh.

Thank you to my dear friends, *mishpacha* Huggins, Ray and Mary Ann, and their sons, Conagher and Sage who sponsor the weekly

Breslov Lunchtime Learning, as well as Ray's mother, our warm-hearted friend Laura Huggins, who learns *emunah* on St. Lawrence Island, in the Bering Sea. Their friendship, generosity and love bring me (and my husband) much joy – and joy is the vital ingredient in our relationship with Hashem. May they be blessed along every step of their journey.

Thanks to Rabbi Dovid Sears of BreslovCenter for answering many questions with kindness and erudition. Thank you to Rabbi Meir Elkabas, for sharing his learning approach with me, laying a foundation for my own learning. Thank you also for always offering powerful inspiration and prayers. Many thanks to Rabbi Elchonon Tauber who has guided me on halachot relevant to teaching diverse groups of students. Thank you to R' Yaakov Klein for creating the Lost Princess Initiative and inviting me to participate in this timely program. I'm grateful to so many great teachers I've learned from including but not limited to: Rav Nissan Dovid Kivak and his weekly lessons; Rav Avraham Tzvi Kluger and his teachings on hisbodedus, Rav Yaakov Meir Shechter, Rav Yitzchok Meir Morgenstern, Rebbetzin Tzipporah Heller, Rebbetzin Yehudis Golshevsky, Rabbi Avraham Sutton, Rabbi Erez Moshe Doron, Rav Yitzchak Ginsburgh, and Rav Moshe Wolfson.

I have so much deep gratitude to Rav Chaim Kramer and his wife Gita, to all their children, and especially their son Tzvi, for dedicating their lives to the spreading of the Rebbe's wisdom. Rabbi Kramer and his father-in-law, Rav Tzvi Aryeh Rosenfeld's commitment to sharing the teachings of Rabbeinu are the reason I and so many thousands of people, are burning with the fire of Breslov. The teaching, writing, and the other projects I have done and am doing for BRI (Breslov Research Institute) for nearly a decade have taught me so much, thank you to Rabbi Kramer for believing in me. Also, the Kramers deserve gratitude and honor for bringing so many people including me to Uman, despite the seemingly relentless obstacles. Gita's strength in the face of tremendous challenges always awes and inspires me. May they always be blessed with good health, simcha, nachas and closeness to the Tzaddik Emes and Hashem.

It was my husband Moshe Chaim ben Chava Josephine, who gave me my first real taste of living life illuminated by the truth of Rabbeinu zal's teachings. He is my rabbi, my inspiration and best friend. May he be blessed to experience revealed (and other) blessings, good health, nachas and a good, long life rich in spiritual growth.

Thank you to the Tzaddik Emes, Rabbeinu Nachman ben Faiga, your teachings saved my life. Thank you to Hashem for absolutely everything.

Chaya Rivka Zwolinski
Nissan 5780
April 2020

Glossary

Ahavat Yisrael	Hebrew, the mitzvah to love your fellow Jews (individuals and the people/nation of Israel)
Amalek	Heb., the Biblical enemy who brutally attacked the Jewish people, the *Amelekites* were the forbears of Haman; we are commanded to obliterate *Amalek* and never forget what they did to us; Amalek has the same *gematria* as *safek*, doubt (240), which destroys *emunah*
Azamra	Heb., lit. I will sing/make music, refers to Rebbe Nachman's famous lesson in Likutey Moharan, 282, as well as the concept of Azamra described in the lesson – to look for the good point in others and one's self; the Tzaddik "composes" a beautiful melody of these good points

azut d'kedusha	Heb., holy boldness, holy *chutzpah;* the bold-ness necessary to live a life of spiritual growth
bitachon	Heb., trust; living with faith in action – applied *emunah*
bracha	Heb., blessing
Breslov	(various spellings include Bratslav, Breslev, etc.) a small city in Ukraine
Chassidic	movement named by Rebbe Nachman after the town; Rebbe Nachman famously said that BReSLoV has the same letters as LeV BaSaR, a "heart of flesh", (Ezekiel 36:26), referring to the concept of connecting to Hashem with an open heart
chassid/chassidim	Heb., (sing./pl.) lit. a pious person, but today primarily refers to someone who follows *Chassidic* teachings which emphasize prayer, joy, faith, love of God and love of others, etc.
chassidut/chassidus	Heb., (Sephardic/Ashkenazic) the body of teachings of the Chassidic movement in general or a particular Chassidic path (i.e. *Breslov*)
chelek elokim	Heb., a portion or piece of God
chutzpah	Heb., brazenness, impudence
da'at	Heb., in general usage, it means intelligence or knowledge; its deeper meaning is a holy awareness and knowledge of God

daven/davening	Yiddish, common term for pray/praying
emet/emes	Heb., (Sephardic/Ashkenazic) truth
emunah	Heb., faith
Esther	Heb., Queen and niece of Mordechai in the story of Purim, who saved the Jewish people from being destroyed by Haman with her bravery and intelligence with great self-sacrifice
gematria	Heb., the Hebrew language is the holy tongue the Holy One used to create the world, therefore embedded in each word and letter are layers of mystic codes, *gematria* is the name for several systems of determining hidden meanings in the words and letters by numeric code
geula	Heb., world redemption and the arrival of Moshiach
halacha	Heb., related to *halicha* (walking or progressing), it is Jewish codes (often referred to as laws), the details of the *mitzvot* given by the Creator, and the actualization of which strengthen one's spiritual connection to the Creator
Haman	descendant of *Amalek*, the embodiment of evil in the Perisan empire, in the mid-third century, BCE, who tried to destroy Mordechai and the Jewish people (see the Book of *Esther*)

Hashem	Heb., lit., "the name", a way to refer to God by the Holy Name without using the name indiscriminately
havdalah	Heb., *the parting ceremony which concludes Shabbat*
Hashgacha pratit/ Hashgacha pratis	Heb., Sephardic/Ashkenazic pronunciations, Divine Providence, Hashem's never-ending comprehensive, supervision of everything in creation
hitbodedut/ hisbodedus	Heb., Sephardic/Ashkenazic pronunciations, talking to Hashem in your own words, in private, as you would a best friend; prayerful meditation; Rebbe Nachman emphasized the importance of hitbodedut and taught that it was central to achieving spiritual growth
Gehinnom	Heb., the spiritual realm where we are purified after leaving this world
Kabbalah/kabbalist	Heb., The Kabbalah is the name for the wisdom of the mystic, inner Torah, recorded in numerous texts across the centuries; a kabbalist is someone who is immersed in the study and application of Kabbalah
klipah	Heb., lit. husks or peels; usually refers to the spiritual husks of impurity which were a by-product of creation
Likutey Moharan	Heb., (the Collected Teachings of Our Teacher, Rabbi Nachman), Rebbe Nachman's magnum opus, part one (286 lessons) and part two (125 lessons), containing

multi-layered teachings on Jewish mysticism, personal growth, ethics, Jewish practice and law, prayer, and more

Malachim (Seraphim, Chayot, Ophanim)
Heb., Angels (types of angels); energy-beings created to carry out a single mission

Megillat Esther
Heb., The Scroll of Esther, the last book in the *Tanakh*, telling the Purim Story

Melave Malka
Heb., lit. escorting the (Shabbat) Queen; the festive meal (with singing and dancing) Jews celebrate after Havdalah, each Shabbat

menia/meniot
Heb., (sing./pl.) obstacle/obstacles; Rebbe Nachman taught that whenever someone is attempting to do something that will bring him closer to Hashem, especially connecting to/going to see the Tzaddik, meniot will arise

mitzvah/mitzvot
Heb., (sing./pl.) commandment; a mitzvah is one of 613 special pathways created by Hashem with which we can connect to Him and which He commanded us to follow (sometimes colloquially used to mean a "good deed")

Mordechai
Queen Esther's Uncle, the pious Jew who helped save the nation during the events of Purim

Moshe Rebbeinu
Heb., lit. Moses our teacher, the prophet and archetypal Tzaddik who led the Jews out of Egypt and who had great love for the Jewish people

Moshiach/Mashiach	Heb., lit. "the anointed one", the Messiah
nekuda tova	Heb., the "good point" inside each person
neshama	Heb., one of five parts of the soul, the part which is attracted to Hashem; also used to refer to soul in general
Olam HaBa	Heb., lit. the World to Come, Olam HaBa refers to both the afterlife and the time of the geulah and Moshiach
ratzon	Heb., will, yearning, desire
rebbe/rebbeinu/ rabbeinu	Heb., is a spiritual leader, usually Chassidic; rebbeinu refers to "our rebbe"
Ribono shel Olam	Heb., Master of the Universe (God)
ruach	Heb., spirit/wind/part of the soul
ruach hakodesh	Heb., lit. spirit of holiness, refers to having a special insight/foreknowledge
seudah shlishit/ shaleshedes	Heb., Sephardic/Ashkenazic pronunciations, the third meal of Shabbat
Shalom	Heb., peace/hello/goodbye/a name of God
Shechinah	Heb., the hidden, feminine-aspect of Hashem also called the Divine Presence, She is in exile with us and will dwell once again in the times of Moshiach; today, the Shechina remains in one unique place: the Kotel (the Western Wall of the Holy Temple) still standing in Jerusalem

shul	Yid., synagogue
siddur	Heb., prayerbook
simcha	Heb., authentic joy; also refers to a special joyous celebration of a mitzvah such as a wedding
Talmud	Heb., nearly 3000 double-pages long, the Talmud is largely comprised of the Mishna, the Oral Law which was first written down in the 2nd century CE, and the Gemara, rabbinic discussions and commentary; it is the guide for living life as Jew and offers discussions of Jewish law, customs, Jewish thought and ethics, history, stories, and much more, much of Midrash (textual commentary on law and Biblical narrative) is also included
Tehillim	Heb., Psalms, King David wrote and compiled these lyrical poem-songs; a book of the Tanakh
teshuva	Heb., to return to God and one's (true) self and follow the path of Torah; to repent
tikkun/tikkunim	Heb., (sing./pl.) correction, healing, repair
Tikkun Haklali	Heb., lit. Universal/General Remedy/Rectification, a special collection of ten Psalms revealed by Rebbe Nachman which effect a healing and correction of the soul; Breslovers generally recite the Tikkun Haklali at least once a day (see Rebbe Nachman's Tikkun; The Breslov Research Institute)

tochacha	Heb., moral rebuke
Torah	Heb., may refer to the Five Books of Moses and/or the scroll it is written on by a scribe; the Hebrew Bible (Tanakh); the combined texts of Jewish wisdom, especially the Tanakh, the Talmud, and often the Shulchan Aruch (codes of Jewish law) and the Kabbalah; may also include works of Chassidut and Mussar and other teachings; an individual lesson/the body of work of a sage/Tzaddik, especially *Likutey Moharan*
tzaddik/tzaddikim	Heb., (sing./pl.) a highly righteous individual devoted to serving Hashem and helping individuals come closer to Him, the tzaddik has a unique role in Judaism in general, and in Breslov Chassidut in particular
tzaddik emet	Heb., true tzaddik, may refer to Rebbe Nachman or other authentic tzaddikim of great stature; only a true tzaddik knows what a person needs to do complete teshuvah
tzedakah	Heb., lit. justice, usually refers to charity which is considered a moral obligation in Judaism, Jews give a minimum of ten percent of their income to tzedakah, Breslovers often give twenty percent. Tzedakah is seen as the holy way to distribute the monetary and other gifts that Hashem bestows upon an invidiual
yetzer hara	Heb., evil inclination, usually refers to an innate negative desire or inclination which can be overcome with prayer, learning and will but it may also refer to a negative

occurrence which tries to prevent one from coming closer to Hashem

yishuv hadaat   Heb., a settled mind, peace of mind, equanimity

zayde   Yid., grandfather

zerizut   Heb., usually referring to enthusiasm and alacrity in religious and spiritual matters

Zohar   Heb., lit. radiance or splendor, the most studied Kabbalistic text, written by Shimon bar Yochai in the 2nd century, CE, it contains mystic discussions of God and creation, the nature of the soul, good and evil, and much more

Biographies

Rebbe Nachman of Breslov

Rebbe Nachman was born in 1772 in Mezhibuzh, Ukraine in the home of his great grandfather, the Baal Shem Tov, founder of the Chasidic movement. The fresh approach of Chasidut revived ancient Jewish concepts that had gone into hibernation throughout much of the diaspora, concepts such as: joy's essential role in personal spiritual service; the Holy One's love and compassion for even the simplest person; the importance developing a relationship with Hashem; and many other life-changing teachings. From his earliest childhood Rebbe Nachman, a unique thinker extraordinaire, embraced these concepts and began to bring forth numerous new ones, forming a body of work unmatched in intellectual and spiritual depth and breadth. The teachings of Rebbe Nachman and his early followers are as fresh and relevant today as they were two centuries ago. His lessons are passionately conveyed through brilliant intellectual explorations of virtually every topic in Judaism, deep mystical revelations, and unique pairings of themes and ideas; fascinating stories that veil great Kabbalistic ideas; and powerful practical advice. Rebbe Nachman passed from this world in 1810, but two centuries later, more and more people continue to attach themselves to him through visiting his resting place in Uman, Ukraine and studying, meditating on and applying his wisdom. Those that do, find solace in their struggles and relief from heartache, doubts and confusion. Most of all, his teachings strengthen our faith and help us live lives of joy – they heal the soul.

Reb Noson

Reb Noson Sternhartz, born in 1780 in Nemirov, Ukraine, was a great Jewish scholar and spiritual seeker. Yearning to become closer to Hashem, he sought answers from the Chassidic mystics and eventually found Rebbe Nachman. He became the Rebbe's student during the last eight years of the Rebbe's life. Reb Noson was Rebbe Nachman's main scribe and most important follower, and according to the Rebbe himself, the primary reason why the Rebbe's works were published and distributed. Reb Noson devoted his life until his death in 1844 to spreading Breslov Chassidut, despite tremendous hardship. He was also the prolific author of numerous original works of halacha, prayers, Kabbalah, and letters, which were based on or referenced the Rebbe's teachings, and are scholarly and inspirational masterpieces in their own right.

Baal Shem Tov

Yisrael ben Eliezer, born in 1698 in Ukraine, is known as the Baal Shem Tov (Master of the Good Name.) He was a rabbi, healer, mystic, and founder of the Chassidic movement, and Rebbe Nachman's great grandfather. (His daughter Udel was the mother of Rebbe Nachman's mother, Fayge.) He was orphaned at a young age and became a teacher of young children. The Jews were suffering under the anti-Semitism of the Church-incited pogroms and as well as massacres by various nationalist and other groups, sometimes including their close neighbors, and they lived with constant fear. Adding to that was a high infant mortality rate, rampant disease and poverty – it was a difficult time to be alive. Itinerant Jewish preachers used to travel to synagogues and chastise the congregations to repent, shaming, scolding and frightening them. The Baal Shem Tov changed this practice, saying it was the wrong way to bring people closer to Hashem, when they were already suffering so much. The Baal Shem Tov revolutionized the Judaism of his time and place and the movement he founded is continuing to grow and inspire people now in the 21st century.

Made in the USA
Middletown, DE
26 January 2023

23258230R00156